A PILLAR OF STRENGTH
IN THE PIT OF HELL...

Ian had been in France for the British secret service before the war. His wife was French. In an ambush in Paris in 1942 his wife was shot and he was captured.

Ian was fantastic. They had pulled most of his teeth and he had cigarette burns over his whole body, but he was the furthest thing from "broken." He lashed out at the guards and the capos. He even scared the SS. His habit was to shout at them, call them swine and tell them he would hang them all. "Yes, after the war ... *schhwwwekkk*" — with gestures and the sound effects of garrotting he made sure the SS got his message. Then he would start into "God Save the King." Whether he knew they wouldn't kill him or just didn't care, he was incredible. With Ian around it was easy to be damn near as brave as he was....

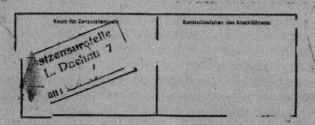

NIGHT AND FOG

A SURVIVOR'S STORY

Arne Brun Lie

WITH ROBBY ROBINSON

BERKLEY BOOKS, NEW YORK

This Berkley book contains the complete
text of the original hardcover edition.

NIGHT AND FOG

A Berkley Book / published by arrangement with
W. W. Norton & Company

PRINTING HISTORY
W. W. Norton & Company edition / January 1990
Berkley edition / September 1992

ISBN: 0-425-13404-0

A BERKLEY BOOK ® TM 757,375
Berkley Books are published by The Berkley Publishing Group,
200 Madison Avenue, New York, New York 10016.
The name "BERKLEY" and the "B" logo
are trademarks belonging to Berkley Publishing Corporation.

PRINTED IN THE UNITED STATES OF AMERICA

10 9 8 7 6 5 4 3 2 1

To my wife, Ellen

Acknowledgments

I am indebted to Kathy and Chris Knight for encouragement from the very beginning of my writing, and later, for advice to both Robby and myself.

I would also like to thank my cousin Naomie Lee Hamilton for help, my sister Sylvei, my crew Tone and Chris, and, in particular, Elie Wiesel for his help and guidance.

Night and Fog

Chapter One

In the camps, we dreamed of elephants . . . elephants breaking down walls and trampling barbed wire . . . elephants slapping aside guard dogs, elephants tramping on SS guards. We dreamed of elephants breaking us free from cabbage-water soup, from living in our own filth, from watching friends waste away. We dreamed of standing like mountains that the Nazis couldn't move. We dreamed of going where they couldn't stop us.

In the camps I had a number but no name. I had a steel bowl, a wooden spoon, and a striped prison uniform. That's all that any of us had. That and some dreams. We dreamed of elephants and having the strength to change things. We dreamed of meat pie and thick gravy. We dreamed we might wake up from our nightmare to rediscover warmth. We dreamed we could walk away from this hell where joy and kindness were ghosts and death was as everyday as breathing—and sometimes easier. In the camps we had wonderful, desperate, distracting dreams, dreams to take strength from, to fly on, to warm up with. In the camps we dreamed of elephants.

My "escape dream" wasn't a plan to fly over the wires or tunnel beneath the walls. Escapes from the Nazi system of *Konzentrationslager und Vernichtungslager*—concentration and extermination camps—were very rare. For one thing, there were automatic reprisals. If there was an escape, successful or not, the Nazis killed ten prisoners for every prisoner involved. The big reason why most of us never tried to escape, though, was the life in the camps. It was the routine—the way we were broken down and degraded. Our daily diet of one bowl of coffee surrogate, a slice of bread, and cabbage-water soup. We were robbed of the energy to escape. But suppose you did escape: How could you hide the "prison look" from the Nazis? Even on the other side of the wire, our sunken eyes, shaved skulls, and emaciated bodies would be giveaways to anyone who saw us. Escapes require shelter, help, rescue. We had no help, because we were *Nacht und Nebel*, night and fog, and no one even knew we were alive. Toward the end of my year in the camps, I made a brief, desperate plan to escape, but my survival was due not so much to escape as to an escape dream.

We all needed a lifeline to help us hang on to ourselves. For me, the lifeline was dreams . . . dreams of sailing.

I used memories of sailboats and sailing like sugar candies to take away the bitterness of life in the camps. The freedom, the exhilaration, the fulfillment of sailing was an antidote to the clenched humiliation of being a prisoner. The more the SS bore down, the more the Gestapo took away, the more I invested in my sea dreams. I survived. I outlasted the camps. That I lived to be rescued, that I was alive enough to be returned at the war's end to Norway, I owe to luck and to those dreams.

I am still a sailor. In 1981 some of my sea dreams came true. I sailed my boat, the thirty-seven-foot cutter *Tresbelle*, from Boston across the Atlantic to Oslo. It was my sternest test as a skipper. I needed all I'd learned of sailing and more. That odyssey across the ocean also put me face to face with my year in the concentration camps. For nearly forty years, it had been in my mind and dreams. On the ocean trip, though, I finally found myself free to confront it, free to try to think and feel what it meant. The voyage of *Tresbelle* from Boston to Oslo was the beginning of this book.

About twenty years after the war, I began having nightmares about the camps, and especially about the execution of my three friends from school. They unlocked a closet that I had tried to close forever. To lead a normal life, I had done my best to keep that closet closed. My transatlantic odyssey in *Tresbelle* was a break from normal life, and it also broke my habit of keeping my foot against the door. At last I went into the closet and dragged forth what I could. This book is the story of what I found. The realities of the concentration camps and the sea for me are connected. What courage and clarity I bring to telling my survivor's tale I feel I owe to over six decades of "seatime." What I love in the sea I treasure more deeply thanks to the camps.

Surfacing through dreamless sleep came in stages, such as a diver goes through decompressing. I was a long way from breaking free, but a strange sound swam into my mind. I had worn myself into exhaustion and deep sleep. Now, partly out of it I heard:

Tapok-ka-pok . . . *tapok-ka-pok* . . . *tapok-ka-pok.* Rhythmic, insistent, like wheezing or underwater burbling or thick silk being torn slowly. I had no idea . . .

"Wake up! Wake up! Arne, for God's sake, wake up!"

My mother. I'd never heard her say, "for God's sake" before.

The light was on. I couldn't see beyond it. In the glare I made out men, silhouettes of men, men in boots. I could hear men speaking Norwegian. But I could still hear.

Tapok-ka-pok . . . *tapok-ka-pok* . . .

The men at my door, in my room, had Sten guns. In the Resistance, we trained with Sten guns. Resistance guys! They must need me. They need me. The raid? They must need me for the raid.

I was waking bit by bit. I started to get out of bed.

"I'm coming, I'm coming. I'll be right with you."

I swung out of my covers to look for my trousers.

My Resistance group was going on a raid that night. The Nazis planned to mobilize young Norwegians into the Waffen SS and send them to the Eastern Front. For this they needed the records of the *Arbeitsdienst,* the labor service. Some of these work records were kept in a flat near us in suburban Oslo. Orders had come from London: we were to break into the flat and burn the files.

I was not far enough along in training to go on the raid. That's why earlier I hadn't been able to get to sleep. My friends were there. I wanted to be there. I didn't want to be worrying in my bed. Finally I had fallen asleep, exhausted, and now I almost couldn't wake up.

Something must have happened. They must need me.

One of the men grabbed me. "Stand still, you little bastard."

What? Who are you? What the hell?

Then I saw the armband, the symbol, the twisted mix of stylized swastika and Viking cross . . . the Norwegian Nazi symbol. These guys were Stapo . . . Norwegian Nazi police. They worked with the Gestapo. The Stapo carried Sten guns, too.

I glared at my mother and father and thought: "Why did you let them in? Why didn't you let me know?"

"You are caught, Jøssing." (The Nazis called us Jøssings because the *Altmark* incident, one of the "provocations" for the German invasion, took place in the Jøssingfjord.)

"Come with us. Now!"

My family didn't know anything about my Resistance work, but they seemed not to be surprised. In occupied Norway, it was not so unusual for people to be snatched from their beds at two or three in the morning. I could see Kirsten, my sister, standing quietly off to one side. Her mouth was set, her eyes sparking. I knew she was trying to think of something, trying to distract the police.

Then I saw Mette or at least her nose and eyes, all that poked out from under my bed. She weighed over a hundred pounds. Reisenschanuzers are excellent sledge dogs but wild. She had bitten my father and my sister. She'd killed two terriers. What was she doing cowering under my bed?

I hoped she'd burst out at the police, let me get away. Her whimpers of fear made that seem unlikely.

My father, calmly, politely, told the policemen that there was obviously a mistake, that his son was not a Resistance fighter, that there were hundreds of families named Lie in Oslo and that they undoubtedly had the wrong one, that—

"Enough! Shut up!" a Stapo said.

Who were these goons with Sten guns to come into my home this way? One stood fixed in the doorway as if on sentry duty. Another roamed my room, gesturing and jerking with his weapon. The one closest to me kept looking around as if he expected another freedom fighter to come jumping out of the closet. These Stapo were very nervous. For all they knew they'd been sent to arrest a dangerous Resistance fighter. If I'd been a few more weeks into my training, if the dog had been a bit braver, they might have had their hands full. But I had no weapon, no escape route, no planned diversion. All I could do was yield.

When they bullied my father, it infuriated me. I was about to speak up. Then the same weird sucking, coughing, clacking noise surfaced again. It made me wonder if this wasn't some sort of dream, a nightmare sparked by worrying over the raid. Then a Stapo stepped hard on my bare toes with his boot. He hissed, "That is enough. Just come with us."

He ground his foot on mine. Another one had my arms

pinned. I felt like a netted fish. The pain in my foot was bad. Tears in my eyes, I looked for my clothes.

My father and sister tried to delay the arrest, but they couldn't. My mother at least succeeded in getting them to let me put my pants on.

"Goodbye. Don't worry." That's all I could say.

At the bottom of the stairs I saw the splintered doorframe. They had broken the door in. Sons of bitches! Who did they think they were? My father's home! My home! I didn't know where they were taking me, but it all was unfair, incredibly unfair.

Maybe that was all these "play" soldiers were good at . . . catching an unarmed teenage kid in his bedroom, bravely poking him with their guns to make the most of their victory. Besides dropping some anti-Nazi leaflets near a German barracks, I hadn't done anything.

My righteous indignation and the fact that I didn't know what else to do made me resolve just to deny everything. How much could they know about me, anyway? They were treating me like a master spy or a threat to the Reich. But why had they come for me? Had someone in my group broken down? Had they been trailing us during training? Claiming innocence, that was my best chance . . . saying I was innocent of everything.

The police van! That godawful *Tapok-ka-pok* noise that had been gnawing away in my head came from the police van. It was a converted truck. The Stapo had this limping, wheezing truck, and their driver must have been afraid to shut it off while they were arresting me because he probably wouldn't be able to get it started again. It had one of those engines converted to run on wood gas. Next time the clowns came for me I'd know the sound and be gone out the window.

The trip to Stapo headquarters didn't take long. I felt cold and very much alone. My family, my friends, my Resistance group—no one could help me. I sat shivering in the emptiness of the van, alone with four Stapo.

I was lost, wondering what had happened, wondering what would happen, trying to steel myself for whatever it was. I'd been living under Nazi rule almost four years. First, Wehrmacht, the regular army. They were almost all gone now. The Nazi storm troops, the SS, were still around, though, wearing their death's-heads and their snotty looks. There were the Gestapo, or secret police. They were the full-time cops. I had never had anything to do with any of them, even the Stapo. My resistance had so far been pitifully slight and unsuccessful, but still, I knew these bastards had shot people for less. If they found that I was working with an action group, armed and directed by the king's government exiled in London, what would they do then?

"How do you think they will taste?"

"Pardon?" I was surprised when the soldier next to me spoke in a near-friendly tone.

The soldier on my other side repeated, "How do you think they will taste?"

"What?"

"How do you think your balls will taste when we cut them off and shove them down your throat?" cackled the first one. Nazis were such nice people.

My guards got tenser and more aggressive as we came closer to headquarters. They poked fun at me, tried to scare me (which they should have seen was unnecessary), jostled me, jabbed me. When we arrived, they ran me right inside. The Stapo were quartered in a drab building, paint cracking on the woodwork, overheated, dusty, puddles of melted snow on the floor, mud tracked across the main foyer. There was a big picture of Quisling on the wall across from the entry door. My guards drew me up in front of it.

"OK, you little weasel. Salute! Respect your leader. Salute! Heil Quisling!"

Maybe it was not really a choice, maybe there wouldn't have been any difference in how they treated me if I'd saluted. But at that point, it came to me that my "innocence" was no protection at all against them. They might just be bluffing, but if they knew enough to arrest me in the first place, then they would know enough to shoot holes in my story. It may have been foolish, but when they ordered me again to salute Quisling, I told them, "Go to hell."

Right there, in the open hallway, the beating started. First two soldiers beat me with their fists and kicked at me with their boots while the others held me.

"Pig! Traitor! Shit! Scum!"

They screamed and cursed as they hit me and kicked me. I tried to duck and roll my head and protect myself. I was surprised.

I can take this, I thought. There were no bones cracking, and I still had my balls. Peaks of pain stood out of the *whomp-ugh-whap* rhythm of the beating, but I thought, I can take this . . . I'm going to make it.

Then they kicked me into a room. Someone new must have taken over the beating. Fewer curses and more questions. Two of them held me on a stool. The others took turns flogging me across the back. They were using wrist-thick ropes and coming down with two-handed swings as if they were splitting wood. I guess they knocked me off the stool onto the floor. I tried to stay on the stool so that they couldn't kick me so easily, but I guess they knocked me down. I can remember questions:

"Do you know Jan Naerup?"

"Of course."

"Per Stranger-Thorsen?"

"Yes, they are my classmates. Of course I know them."

"Have you ever seen a limpet mine?"

"A what?"

Fifteen strokes later, "A limpet mine?"

We had trained with limpet mines and hand grenades and Sten guns. Yes, the edge of my hand was calloused and tough from karate training, breaking boards. I think I denied all of this at first, but then I passed out. They revived me, beat me, revived me, questioned me. Now I knew I couldn't bear it. I couldn't. It hurt. It hurt so badly. It hurt all over. It had to stop. I just wanted it to stop.

"Okay, I confess! I killed my father! I did it, whatever it is! Just stop!"

But they didn't stop. All through the rest of the night. All through endless minutes—hours? days? They beat me, questioned me, beat me, revived me, questioned me. The little that I really knew ceased to interest them except, I figured out, the one piece of the puzzle that they still didn't have.

"Who engaged you? Who was your contact to get into the Resistance?"

Jan Naerup had been my contact. I thought I had heard them bringing him in, so I tried to cover for him. I told them that I was the contact.

"He lies!"

Over and over the pattern was repeated. Same question, same answer; more strokes with two-inch hawsers. When they finally gave me my "confession" to sign, I felt I'd won a victory. At least the beating stopped. The next thing I remember was being hustled from a cell block down to the main hall of the Stapo headquarters. Other prisoners were ranged around the walls, face to the wall, with hands splayed out in front of them over their heads. They threw me against the wall between two other bloodied men.

I couldn't believe my eyes! Standing right next to me in this hellhole police station was Ragnvald Flakstad, from school. Ragnvald sat next to me in school. What the hell was he doing here? He'd been beaten. What on earth? We weren't close friends, but throughout our school career we'd been classmates. What the hell was he doing here?

I caught his eye. He stood maybe two inches taller than I but now he seemed much shorter. Behind flecks of pain, I saw surprise when he recognized me. I couldn't tell at once why he looked so strange. His leg! I saw that he was standing on one foot while his other leg dangled dead a few inches off the floor. I was trying to communicate with him, trying to find out, when Jonas Lie strode in.

His name is spelled as mine is but I am proud that we are not related. It's funny. One of Norway's famous authors from the last century, as famous in Norway as Hamsun or even Ibsen, was Jonas Lie. I used to joke that I wasn't from the literary branch of my family. I wonder about Jonas. It's hard to imagine him joking about anything.

Lie was chief of the Stapo. In wartime Oslo there were few men more feared and hated. Unlike Quisling, whom even his own people knew to be a weak-chinned opportunist, Lie was strong and tough. He gave the Stapo discipline enough so that they played a big role in policing Norway for the Nazis. He looked like a Nazi. He had spotless black jackboots even though it was a mess of mud outside in the streets. He had a barrel chest and an upright bearing that reminded one of a well-trained bear.

He spoke with a curiously soft voice: "You have ruined your lives. I don't know why you chose to throw away your lives when you are so young. You might have joined us in building the new order, in pushing ahead. Such mindless violence and disrespect of authority as you have shown are unthinkable. You chose sneaking, breaking and entry, arson, and wanton shooting in peaceable neighborhoods. You have accomplished nothing except to ruin your lives. It is my small regret that you will not live to see the day when the order is completely in place, throughout Norway and the rest of the world."

I was facing the wall, but by turning my head slightly I could see the great chief as he spoke. Could he possibly take those words seriously? That we were breaking the law when he was collaborating with the Nazi invaders? The hypocrisy, the half-truths, the out-and-out lies. Why did these guys need to lie like that? Did they really need to be propped up by all this rhetorical crap so they could pillage and torture and steal?

Throughout the days to come in the camps, throughout my life under occupation, I heard words like those over and over again. They must make some kind of sense, but they are hollow, so hollow. I still wonder about Jonas Lie, strutting back and forth in the entry hall, keeping a soldier, drawn gun on the table, between himself and killers like me. Was there an ounce of honesty in the man? Was there a postage stamp of soul to respect?

After Lie addressed us, we were transferred to Akershus Castle, a twelfth-century fortress in the middle of Oslo, a dungeon run by the Wehrmacht. There was very little left of me, certainly not much of my sense of humor, but I was almost able to laugh when they threw my beaten remains in a cell and hung a red-lettered sign outside: *Sehr gefährlicher Häftling*. Very dangerous prisoner.

Chapter Two

It hurt to move. The view from my slit window was of a rough stone wall on the other side of a kind of alleyway inside the castle. I didn't know how long I'd slept. It hurt to move at all, but I limped and crawled around my tiny space. The floor was wooden. The walls were wooden. I had only the view from the window slit. My cell door opened onto another corridor. There was one hole at the base of a wall.

I'd been warned about double agents, but I wanted to know what had happened to my group, to my friends. I whispered at the hole but there was no response. I had a terrible need to talk. I would have talked to the Gestapo chief if he had come to listen. I had been snatched from my bed and my life, all orderly and clear, into this threshing machine of beatings and lectures and beatings and being rousted. I wondered if I still existed. I wanted to talk to someone, but there was no one, so I went back to sleep.

Later I learned Ragnvald was only three cells away.

I remember that first time in Akershus. The guards came by often, but not often enough to keep us from chain-whispering. Ragnvald, I found out by hissed bits passed along to me, was working in Mil-Org (Military Organization) D-13. My group was an "action group" designed for sabotage. Mil-Org was supposed to prepare a military uprising. Ragnvald had heard about a firefight of some kind with the Stapo. He was always so serious. It was just like him to think he was supposed to be "doing something" and to report to his commander. When he did, the men of the SD—a branch of the Gestapo—were there to grab him. I wonder what kind of look was on Ragnvald's pudgy poker face when they did.

"What the hell happened last night?" we asked each other up and down our chill corridor.

Across the little street between rows of cells was Jan Naerup. He hadn't been at the raid but he'd been rounded up. How much did they know about us? Ragnvald was in the Resistance. He sat next to me in school and I had had no idea that he was involved. Neither one of us knew about the other, but those bastards in the Stapo knew about us both. You had to give them credit.

My efforts to cover Jan convinced them that I knew more than I really did. Even though I'd already "confessed," the next day I was taken to Gestapo headquarters. Waiting alone in my cell in the dark basement of Viktoria Terrasse, I was truly scared. The beating that my own countrymen had given me was still very much with me. I had stiffened up and couldn't move at all without hurting. How much worse would it be from the masters of torture? All of those stories, about bones being cracked, cigarette tortures, ice baths, injections, nail pullings, went through my mind. Granted, some didn't even sound so bad compared to what the Stapo had done to me, but I was very tender and very scared. A taste like steel in my mouth, my stomach filled with lead, I was sweating and shivering and feeling terribly sorry for myself all at the same time.

I learned from Ragnvald what they'd done to him, and that scared me more. They had put "twinges," a sort of vise, on either end of his calf muscle. Then they had jolted his leg out straight, breaking the muscle in two. He didn't complain, but my God . . . would a muscle broken that way ever heal?

They fetched me at last. At least the waiting was over. There were three: two Gestapo and a Norwegian translator. They brought me into a small office on one of the upper floors of the old building. I don't think they even closed the door. "Who engaged you to fight against the Reich?" I told them, with some elaboration, the same story I had told the Stapo. "Er lügt!"—He lies!

I'm not sure whether both men hit me at the same time but the next thing I knew, I was facedown on the floor. My head was spinning. I felt my stomach rise into my throat. I wasn't sick, but I couldn't speak.

"Take him back to his cell."

I couldn't believe my luck. Last night they had beaten me for hours. Could this be true? Would they really take me back to Akershus? To my great surprise, they did.

Whispering at night, I was able to learn a bit more. Jon Hatland, Per Stranger-Thorsen, and Lars Eriksen, my three friends, the three who had gone on the raid, had been arrested. The sabotage must have been bungled somehow.

The days in Akershus were a kind of blur. Locked in . . . let out . . . fed . . . always hoping to learn more, always fearing that they'd beat you more. But one day stands out clearly in my mind. It was Constitution Day, May 17, our national day in Norway. It commemorates the Constitution of 1814 and Norway's freedom after four hundred years of Danish rule.

Holiday or no holiday, we had to urinate. One at a time, the guards would take us out. They didn't like the duty. "Los, los, los, Mensch!" Behind me my keeper prodded. I was used to it, but it never ceased to bother me.

"*Los . . . los, schnell!*" Poking, prodding, running behind me with his rifle, my guard prodded me down to the pissoir. It was just an alcove where we urinated on the wall. The wall was brownish-red because so many of us were passing blood.

"*Los, los, schnell!*" From the other direction came another guard. The prisoner he was pushing was limping. It was Ragnvald.

We reached the wall at about the same time. The stench was sickening, as usual. I looked down to see how Ragnvald's foot was.

It simply dragged there, not even solid enough for him to push off when he walked. It was almost like hopping, the way he moved. He looked worse than I did; yellowish bruises were on his face among swollen welts of red and blue. Up from the middle of all of that I caught what I thought was a wink.

"*Pinkeln! Pinkeln schnell!*"— Piss! Piss quickly! The bastards wouldn't let up for a minute. Didn't they realize that I could piss a lot quicker if they let me alone? All of their shouting made me so nervous I felt as if I half swallowed my urine.

"*Pinkeln! Pinkeln!*"

I started to let fly at last. Ragnvald, too. I looked out through a slit in the wall. Green trees, May sunshine . . . Constitution Day. I caught Ragnvald's eye. I started to giggle, and he did too. In a second we were roaring. What a way to be nineteen and just coming of age. What a way to celebrate our freedom as Norwegians. My God!

It amazed me how quickly I started to heal. I was taken back to the Gestapo once or twice more. They always beat me, but never hard or long. I didn't know whether they believed me or not but I stuck to my story about being the one that recruited my group. Then, one afternoon, they took me to an office in Akershus. There was a German in civilian clothes. He had on a black tie. I don't know if he was really a clergyman or just meant to remind me of one. He asked me how I was being treated in prison. He seemed very friendly. Finally he asked me about my family. Would I like to send them a farewell letter?

The Nazis were not novices at their game. More than the speeches from Jonas Lie, more than the beatings with the hawsers, more than the throat-cutting signs that my SD guards continued to make whenever they could catch my eye, this "kindness" from a "pastor" convinced me that I was doomed. I can't imagine being more scared. However, I never considered taking the paper to write a farewell letter.

That night, soup was served in aluminum casseroles. I kept mine. I looked around and was surprised to find a rusty nail wedged in a crack under the bench in my cell. I wondered if this was really the kind of "pen" supposed to be mightier than the sword. Supper over, the guards, pacing outside, I engraved my supper plate with a few lines from the *Edda*, the great Norse saga.

> Døyr fe
> Døyr frendar
> Eg veit eit som aldri, døyr
> Domen om kvarein død.

The *Edda* is made up of the poems and songs of the warrior kings and voyagers. It comes from the time between myth and history. To be Norse is to know the *Edda*; I had learned these lines in school. They mean:

> Cattle die
> Friends die
> I know something that never dies
> The story about how you die.

I wonder if I had any choice. I knew there was no one to cry to. I knew that I had little or no hope of escaping. I wonder if I'd had a chance to sell my soul what I might have done. I don't know. What I actually did was write those prideful words from the *Edda*. In spite of my dreadful fear, I wanted to make a mark, to leave something behind.

And then I began to think not so much about the story of my own death but about the length of my own life. I thought of my family, of the friends that were with me and the ones who were not, of the places that I loved, of the foods, the girls. And I wondered why I had to die.

There were not any happy answers. Those things that made my life good were sure to be killed by the Nazis. Even that didn't make it all right for me to die. I couldn't let my life just drift away. To hell with it, I thought. I'm just not going to die.

There wasn't much reason for bravery. The cutthroat realities of this execution chamber were still the same, but mourning my own death seemed like giving in to it, like causing it. "Even if there's no reason, I've got to be brave," I muttered to myself.

"Got to be brave."

How many times in my life had I said that to myself? How many times had I heard it from my parents? Of course, we've got to be brave. Got to be brave.

And there popped into my head a scene—my little Colin Archer sailboat model, the one I got for Christmas when I was eight years old, bravely sailing. She was beating into waves almost twice her size, laid flat on her side by each wave and then, twisting, lifting, popping, shivering, on her feet again. Another roller, another puff, and she'd be laid back down. The image was as clear as a movie. The little cutter was not making any headway, but not being carried toward the rocks either. Holding her own.

If I was looking for something to spit in the face of the Gestapo, the quote from the *Edda* was what I needed. Defiant yet stoical, cryptic . . . one hell of an epitaph. But maybe I wasn't ready to bury myself. Sailors in the sagas could run before storms or sink. I didn't know where I could run. "Be brave" . . . but I had no place to run. I won't sink, I told myself. I'll hold my own. Batten down, hang on. Be brave.

Thinking of death took the bottom of my stomach out. I thought of the little cutter, bobbing, slapped down, bobbing up. I thought of the Christmas Day when I got her, and then of ships, skiffs, sailboats, voyages. My raw back against the wall of my cell, I waited for the sound of boots approaching, and I reviewed the boats of my life. Almost like a rosary, I felt over them, saw them, counted them, remembered them.

Before the model sailboat came our play canoe. Sylvei was eight. The album snapshot of us playing then catches her wise, cock-eyed smile, her blond hair, her big, big eyes. I was only three, but I have memories, some sharp, like the broken look of my legs seen through the clear water. Standing calf-deep in the Hardangerfjord, we caught brown crabs and snails. I can see and even hear the fine train of bubbles that our wood-and-canvas canoe trailed behind as I pushed her. Lying in tide pools, facedown, urinating because it felt so warm and good, so free; I can remember that, too.

After the canoe came the little model cutter. She was white. I learned to rig her so she would sail a straight line. My father warned me that changes in the wind would make her change her helm. Then one day she headed off on her own, doubled the point where I was standing and made straight out into the open fjord. I couldn't swim after her. She was sailing out over my head. I hated to call my father, but I also hated to lose my little boat. Dragged from his garden, father was grumpy and made me wait alone on the sand while he rowed out after the model. Half an hour later they returned.

A little while after he rescued the Colin Archer cutter, father made a "land yacht" for us. She was a couple of old packing crates dug into the sand near the Hardangerfjord beach. She had a very impressive mast and boom made out of clothesline poles and a square sail made from an old sack. We would climb and play on her. We fought over the rights to command

and where we were going, but sometimes we would all get caught up in the same adventure. The deck was splintery when we started, but we used the boat so much we wore it smooth.

My father loved his garden more than he did the ocean, but everyone in Norway is connected with the sea. We lived on an island in the Oslofjord much of the time I was growing up. Father went off to work every day, as did all of our neighbors, and when the "poppa boats," the commuting ferries to Oslo, came back to the island at night, it was always the same . . . the children at the dock welcoming their fathers as though they'd been on a three-year voyage.

During those days we did a lot of voyaging. The fjord is full of rocky islets we call "skerries." Where some children have bicycles, we had skiffs and open sailboats to knock about in the skerries. Exploring, fishing, musseling . . . ah yes, pick the mussels from underwater, clean them a bit, put them in a bucket, steam them over a fire, a fire of sizzling half-dry drift-wood burning rainbow flames, or thick with the creosote smog of burning tar, and then of course, eat them. Squalls came off the open fjord. We'd see them coming but sometimes we got caught in them anyway. The seawater seemed warmer than the rain, and we never worried much. If you swamped a boat, we just stuck with it until the wind died down, bailed her out, swam her ashore. Our mothers, though, seemed much more concerned about our adventures.

Thinking of the skerries and those summers, I felt like a caged bird. Had I ever really known how to fly? Had I ever been that free? That happy?

The first time I went to sea was with the Sea Scouts in 1938. The scouts had a lovely black ketch, *Mohawk*, sixty feet long and every inch our dream of a sailing ship. She was glorious to steer, all controlled power as she reached along in a good breeze. The driving whoosh of her bow as it split the waves made you feel she could take you anywhere. Our big expedi-tion that year was a cruise to Sweden. I had heard things ("They drive on the left-hand side of the road and eat chocolate with every meal") from my father and I was excited to be voyaging there.

On our way across, we encountered a gale. My first worry was getting seasick. I felt bad, but I stayed on deck, even when I wasn't on watch, and I concentrated on trimming sails and helping do the work. That saved me. I was proud to retain my breakfast through my first storm at sea. The waves were much bigger than any I'd ever seen. I began to wonder what would happen if we sank. Despite our life jackets and radio I couldn't imagine anyone saving us. Only the ship was taking care of us, and we had damn well better take care of her.

The wind and waves seemed to be lightening up, and I thought that I saw some light behind the low clouds. That's when the watch captain sent me below to check the bilge. It was slopping up over the floorboards. When I told him, he sent me back to pump. The bilge water was greasy and full of bits of bread. The bread would clog the strainer so I had to pump and clear, pump and clear. By the time I was relieved at the pump, the water level was back below the floorboards.

It was raining again when I went on deck. I was chilled after the hot clammy work in the bilge. I remember, though, after work and fear, noticing the beauty of the hiss of the rain on the backs of the rollers as we charged through them.

On the way home, we anchored off the coast. No one seemed to know why until the moon rose and first-time voyagers were all baptized by King Neptune, sitting sternly on his throne in the saloon. From behind his dishmop beard he gave orders, and we were each given a spoonful of foul-tasting medicine "to cure the remainder of our landlubber disease." We knelt before the throne, took off our shirts, and shivered as a silver anchor was painted on our backs. Then, tied by our waists, we were thrown into the sea. Those who survived received elaborate certificates stitched with marlin and signed by Neptune and "his secretary, the Octopus."

Crown Prince Olav raced a gorgeous green eight-meter, *Sira*. She was designed and built by Johan Anker, who had a string of successful designs in several racing classes. Even just riding at her mooring, she would lift and bury in near-perfect harmony and point dead straight into the wind without any yawing or fussing. When the Nazis came, Gauleiter Terboven, the governor installed by the Nazis, seized *Sira* for himself. He would sail her around Oslofjord on weekends, giving orders to his Kriegsmarine sailors, sails luffing and half-hoisted. Dr. Julsrud, one of my family's good friends, was sitting one Sunday on his dock with his wife and children when the Gauleiter brought *Sira* sailing close inshore. He ran aground. Our friends laughed. Terboven bellowed for help. Our friends turned their backs. Later that afternoon a detachment of marines landed at the Julsruds' dock. The whole family was taken to prison for six months.

When the guard came in the morning I was not ready, but I was calm. My casserole with its heroic message was on my bench in plain view. The guard took no notice. Who knew what that meant?

What could I do? It was like being taken from my bedroom all over again; I didn't know what to do. He took me to an anteroom and left me there with prisoners I didn't know. He told us not to talk. What good would talking do? Finally a pair of guards came back. They took me with them and put me between them in the backseat of a Mercedes staff car. It was more elegant than the wood-gas-powered truck that had brought me to Akershus. What did that mean? That made me think of the wheezing, raspy *tapok-ka-pok* from that night—how many nights ago? Two weeks? Just two? To mark the days I had the dried welts and scabs I could see on my hands and wrists in front of me. These days are like blood blisters, I mused. A string of blue-black blood sausages just bursting to pop. No counting off comfort, no calming the mind, no rosary . . . just *saucisses*. . . . Are they now going to break the chain?

We arrived. It was the Höhere SS Polizeigericht, Nord, the higher police tribunal. Throughout the Nazi occupation this was known as a place of no return. It was not so much a court of justice or law as an administrative center that let the Reich keep track of whom they were killing and torturing. The tribune was Police General Redeiss. With Terboven he ruled Norway. He looked just as I imagined he would—black boots, riding breeches, SS cap, gloves, death's head insignia of course.

Everyone in the room except for the prisoners was in uniform, Gestapo, one or two Stapo, SS. We all still wore the clothes we'd been wearing when they captured us. The Nazis had appropriated an old villa in Oslo's West End to be their "court." Draped with a red-white-and-black swatika banner, the "bench" was an ornate, carved, heavy-legged table. Redeiss sat behind it against the wall. Wooden chairs of varying sizes were ranked in rows in front of him. There were guards at the two doors and with each group of prisoners. I wondered how we had managed in the old days to get by with just a judge and a bailiff.

It took me some time to notice, through my self-pity, awe, and fear, that the prisoners in front of me were Jon, Lars, and Per. Lars wasn't in my school, but I had last seen Jon and Per at school hours before they went on the raid to destroy the files. I'd heard that they had been captured, but I still had no idea what really had happened. Whatever it was, though, it couldn't have been good. I wiggled forward as close as I dared, behind Jon's head, and coughed. He seemed to recognize me but my guard hissed, *"Ruhe!"*—Quiet!—and we sat there in silence.

Redeiss was busy conferring. We sat there and waited. I thought of trying to get some sort of sign from my friends. There were guards between them, though. The guards at the end of my bench were talking in whispers.

"Look at that one," said the bigger and older of the two. "With that beard, he's a Jesus." The shorter one was strikingly handsome, with white, perfect teeth. Out of the side of his mouth he said, "He'll be going to meet Jesus soon." Then he laughed, haughty, not even much interested, just amused to see the world being wiped clean of us.

I could understand most of the rest of what they said as they went around the room pronouncing sentences. I wondered what they'd make of scared, skinny, blood-caked me, but before they got that far, the great Redeiss stood. He seemed to be staring at each prisoner, to be fixing him in his mind. Finally he said, "We must wait to begin," and sat down again.

The waiting was terrible. I couldn't talk. Everything I heard assured me that death was coming. Everything I did or thought became "my last." And then I felt almost giddy and my thoughts started to float.

Why didn't Mette bark at the Stapo? . . . My father will take my death hardest. . . . The sledge dogs have a way of gumming your wrist. They mean it in fun, but their mouths are never as soft as they think they are. . . . The book of Rudyard Kipling verse in my aunt's library . . . it had a swastika on it . . . Sanskrit symbol of good luck, my uncle said. . . . If you can keep your head while . . . I doubt that I can keep from wetting my pants . . . incontinent . . . a sissy with wet drawers. . . . Remember the warmth of lying in the shallow water and urinating down your leg . . . not down your leg, really, down your middle . . . the first blush of sex at four years old. . . . How many more years . . . my life away . . . pissing my life away . . . maybe in another life . . . the Sanskrit symbol for the good luck . . . lucky enough to have another life?

I snapped back and focused on the kangaroo court around me. I zeroed in on Jon's hand. I can remember those fingers on the piano in our parlor . . . too big for a parlor or a piano, but playing Rachmaninoff as if there were nothing else in the

world. He was opening and closing his hand. Five, four, three.
Was that a message? What? Numbers? I strained to pick it up,
but just then Redeiss stood up.

"*Achtung!*" We all stood up.

"Luncheon recess," and he walked out.

I thought we would stay for our hearing before the tribunal,
but the guards herded us out in random bunches. Per, Jon,
and Lars were in one group; I went with another. There were
vans, we were herded in, and it was back to our cells. The
guards were real bastards about keeping us quiet. I was completely ignorant about what was happening. I'd been arrested
by myself, and I hadn't talked to anyone except for my whispering circle. What did this tribunal charade mean? Had we
been dismissed? Sentenced? I looked across the van at the prisoner opposite me. He'd been there when we arrived. I wondered if he could tell me anything. I caught his eye and raised
an eyebrow in question.

He mouthed the words "to die."

He was telling me his sentence. He was calm; he could have
been on a tram, telling me to get off at the next stop. But then,
what was my sentence? Wasn't this tribunal thing just a formality, and didn't they do whatever they wanted with you? I
wished I'd been able to communicate with my three friends.

A day or two later, I saw them again. Outside my cell I
heard some unusual noise, more than the stamp of boots and
the exchange of German orders. It was a low-level hubbub; it
reminded me of the sound that came across town from the
Bislet Stadium when there was a track and field meet. From
the window I looked down the long alleyway that ran between
the cellblocks. Jon, Per, and Lars were being marched along
by four guards. They seemed to be walking with some diffi-
culty. I wondered if they'd been beaten again. From the way
they were looking up at the cells, waving and giving the thumbs-
up sign, I could tell. The prisoners all along the corridor could
tell, too, and they were cheering them, waving, making noise

enough that I thought the guards would do something. I could tell. They were walking down the alleyway to be shot. I felt my heart stop. They were beneath my cell window. They stopped and looked up. We saw each other. They waved.

"See you later," Jon said.

"Yeah, see you later, Arne," said the other two.

They said it almost as though they would be back by supper, but I knew I would never see them again in this life. The May sunshine they walked through was glorious and warm. I watched them until they were gone. Controlled and calm, they made no show of defiance, but they didn't have to. It was clear to us that they had not been broken, only caught. In the dark of my cell, I had none of their control. Their courage, their friendship, their calm. My chest shrank tight, and I wept . . . for them, for me, for us all.

Chapter Three

The cell door bangs open. I look up through cold blue light. Against it come death's-head silhouettes. I look for Sten guns, but I see just the glitter of perfect teeth. "Come to meet him. Come to meet Jesus."

I try to hide; I try to hide under my arms, under my bed. I close my eyes. I can still see the blue light. I close my eyes tighter. The blue light turns red, reddish-brown. Pissing blood. I hear the sound, *tapok-ka-pok*, like someone sucking dregs out through a straw. The dregs of the blood? The splatter that it makes sends chills through me. The sound is all around me. "Cows die." The farmer killed his cow and hid his daughter inside the carcass. The Nazis never found her. She was never raped. She was saved. In the cow, under the bed, buried in a stack of corpses, I'll fool them. There is oil in here. Diesel oil, gun oil, leather oil, hair oil. I taste the oil in the air, I feel the oil coating the hairs in my nose. Black, booted, oily bastards bringing oil in here? Yesterday it smelled like seaweed.

Am I in the van? What do I taste? Swallow, swallow to save myself, the strings, the gristle, swallow, don't gag. The light is brighter. Bright and white, and I can see my mother looking for my trousers. I have only one leg to my trousers, my foot hangs dead at the bottom of it. How can I walk calmly, how can I wave goodbye? The ditch is there ahead of us. Half full of rotten leaves. Waving, the three are waving. I'll see them later. I'll see you later! Yes . . . I will, but I see dirty blotches of snow still there. Where is this ditch? Is this ditch in Norway? Will they kill me in Norway? Perfect teeth glitter at me. I stomp barefoot on their boots, I slap and snarl and rage at them while their perfect teeth glint. The moans come from far away. I have hurt them. I am bulldozing free. They moan in fear of me as I rage. Has anyone ever been here? Will anyone ever come here? Sylvei? Father? I am held; they have me. But I'll see you later.

Who says, "I know something that never dies"? Hurry, dammit. "*Heraus*," they all say, with their perfect teeth underwater, slow, and faraway. I try to walk. Moaning as my ripped leg refuses my weight. I walk. Are there twinges on my leg? Jon, Per, Lars—just ahead. Ahead. I'll see you. I'll see you. The screams. Who screams? The guards blow the backs of their heads off and push my friends in the ditch. I still hear screams. They are dead and screaming. I am dead and screaming. I am dead. I am screaming. I am not dead. My screams wake me.

My own choked moans of terror have been waking me from this dream for twenty years. I am sweating. It is dark, and there is noise besides the echoes of the screams. There is motion, too. I haven't heard the guns yet. How could their heads be blown open if I haven't heard the guns?

I'm awake and I'm at sea. I'm warm in my berth on *Tresbelle*, and it smells like bacon. It's not even dark now that I roll my head and turtle out from my eiderdown. I still feel those silent screams, but I am not, I can tell, in the ditch. I feel an up-slide, hiss, boom . . . something like that, an easy up-and-over. We must still be reaching. It must not be blowing too hard; the boat's not heeled very much, not much noise, no crashing into waves.

After I wake from that dream, I am always weak, always shaky and happy to be alive. My three friends were led away. I wasn't. Waking up out here in the Atlantic doesn't change any of that. I still want to throw up when I think of them being shot. I am pitifully grateful to be awake . . . pitifully ashamed that I didn't die as they did. But I'm alive, alive to have this horrendous dream every couple of weeks for years. I have other nightmares, but there's something fiendish about the way it works. The one that puts lead on my chest and makes me scream like a half-slaughtered piglet, that's the one selected by my unconscious for reruns.

Maybe Chris and Tone couldn't hear me scream. They're topside and I'm buttoned up in my bunk down here. But someone must have been cooking the bacon. Do they think their old skipper is a loony? Wonderful, the wounds of war. Forty years later. Like a bladder that dribbles on its own, the old man is a bed-wetting basket case. Worse than bed-wetting. A screaming old man.

The quarterberth aboard *Tresbelle* is just aft of the companionway on the starboard side. It's almost like an open box, a coffin, a sedan chair, a steam closet. Pile it up with cushions and bedding and there's not much room for you to get thrown around in a seaway. It's as close to the womb as old guys like me will get. The ventilation's good. It's a near-perfect sea-berth. A good place for screaming.

The hangover from the dream fades eventually. When the quaking and the disgust have gone, it's not that bad in my bunk. It must be 0600 or so. We're headed east, and the sun comes in in spiky horizontal shafts. Most of the cabin is still in shadow. With images of the execution almost gone, I lie still and warm in my eiderdown. I enjoy the surge as *Tresbelle* moves along, with an occasional creak from her rigging. But if Chris or Tone was below cooking breakfast in the middle of my nightmare, if I upset them . . .

If I were Jack London and this were a novel I might have a plot here, the case of the screaming skipper. Jack and Jill, the unsuspecting crew, would be forced to delve into the old man's mysteries to shut him up. Maybe it would be my guilty conscience from killing too many seals? Too many whales? But I'm a tanner, not a writer, and we're dealing here with what really happened. The truth of the matter is that I know Chris and Tone almost as well as I know my own family. And they know me, and now they know that I scream because of nightmares from the war. They've sailed with me before. I don't think I've ever screamed in my sleep before with them on board, but we've talked about it. I wonder if they'll say anything to the old man.

Chris is a journalist. Tone is a writer and artist. Both are Norwegian and in their late twenties. They were, in fact, lovers at one point a couple of years ago.

They're "just friends" now. When I needed crew to help me deliver *Tresbelle* back home to Oslo from the States, they were the ones I was happy to ask, and happily they had the time and wanted to come. Would I have beautiful young friends like Chris and Tone if I were a loony old screaming sea captain?

You would think that life would have a self-respecting kind of rhythm. You would think that quaking from a nightmare could not be replaced in a matter of minutes with warmth and self-satisfaction, with a feeling of good fortune and well-being. For somebody who is lucky enough to have such a wonderful crew and such a beautiful, well-found boat, though, such rhythms seem to be possible.

Tresbelle is a near-perfect seaboat, if I do say so. She's thirty-seven feet long. Sigurd Herbern designed her as a thirty-six-footer. He and I fought over making her thirty-seven-feet instead.

She was handsome as a white-hulled thirty-six-footer, but she's exquisite at thirty-seven feet now that I've lengthened her bow and angled her stem. (Sigurd says that I've ruined his career.) Calling her *Tresbelle*, "very beautiful," is more than just protesting too much to Sigurd, who thinks she's "scarred." It's more, too, than appreciation for those qualities in a boat that can make hearts beat fast, those qualities like her graceful sheer and balanced overhangs and symphony of wood and white that delight my rheumy old eye. It might seem ironic coming from someone who wakes to screams over ugliness and terror but there's something *très belle* about waking up with bacon cooked and a steady wind on the beam two days out of Boston, bound across the Grand Banks and home to Oslo. Don't let me go on about the name. I chose it and I love it.

I roll over and look around the cabin. Three days ago, it was a madhouse of cardboard boxes, tools, clothes, books, charts, and blankets. We were sitting level and relatively secure in the marina basin at the Coast Guard station in Boston Harbor. Now, out of sight of land, cocked at a ten-degree angle and shaken up and down every fifteen seconds, the cabin is much neater. "Stow before you go." That's sailors' wisdom. While we didn't heed it completely, we've taken care to place most of our gear before the sea took care of doing it for us. The tins and boxes and coils and clumps of clothes have all been stashed. A few things, the big box of chocolate bars, for instance, seem poorly stowed to me, but I guess I've relaxed some from my earliest days at sea with the scouts when "ship's inspection" happened twice daily and loose items went over the side.

Hammocks stuffed with clothes, books wedged in their shelves, a picture of *Tresbelle* at the start of the TwoStar race framed on the bulkhead, the navigation drawer jounced half-open, the bacon drained and wedged in place on top of the swinging stove, the matches and a pair of socks sitting on the table amidship, our Tiny Tot heater, cold and resting against the main bulkhead . . . that's our home, and it looks like it might be a comfortable one for the next three weeks.

This is the morning of our third day out. I guess the road that got us here goes all the way back to when my seafaring started again about a year after I was released from the camps. I came home, ate five or six meals a day for weeks, visited, tried to get better, but I was on a decline from the camps that I couldn't stop. It was diagnosed as consumption, then tubercular pleurisy. I went into a sanatorium. It was winter, dark, and I felt sickly and depressed, under a permanent cloud.

In April, Calle Mortensen wrote me a letter. He and some friends (including, I learned Crown Prince Olav) were putting together a consortium to build and race a new six-meter boat. Did I want to join as a crewman? Imagine a consumptive, depressive scarecrow and you've got about the half of how bad I was. Sailing? The doctors wouldn't ever approve. But somehow they did, and from May on in that summer of 1946, I was full-time crewman on a dream boat. There was another Arne aboard, Arne Kamfjord. I think it was our skipper, Henrik Robert, a man much older than we, who eliminated the confusion between us. To me, he said, "You look like walking death. You are so gaunt, those eyes and your face . . . you look so 'Belsen' "—after Bergen-Belsen, one of the most infamous of the Nazi death camps. Before long, I was called Bels. I was embarrassed and confused at first. Both of those feelings have faded, but the name has not. Most of my friends call me Bels today. Death warmed over.

My health and spirits went up, we had some fine racing and even though I managed to make just about every mistake one could make, old Henrik seemed bound to take care of me. When another boat made a mistake he'd say, "I see Bels has been over there." He was a gritty old guy. Once we went offshore on an overnight race. We'd been sailing in our open boat for eighteen hours, serious racing full-time, all concentration. Finally, I asked if we might have something to eat.

"Oh, Bels," he said, "you're always asking about food. Can't you think of anything else?"

That's when I decided that if I ever had a boat, I would be not only skipper but cook. I got a little boat, then a bigger one, and finally, when my business and my family had grown and become established, I went to Sigurd Herbern and had him design *Tresbelle*. I didn't know if I would ever make a transatlantic crossing, but I wanted her to be capable of one.

Sigurd had been my jujitsu instructor in the Resistance. He escaped to Sweden soon after the raid when we all were caught. He was a brilliant man, so smart that lots of people thought he was a little crazy. He openly criticized the Resistance for being amateurish and poorly organized. After the war people thought this was being ungrateful or cantankerous, but he knew all along how far we were from being effective. Sigurd drew for me a racing boat that had a very different bulbed keel and a skeg-hung fin rudder beneath the water, but also the long over-hangs and narrowish beam of our Scandinavian-style boats. She is an original, but she's drawn from several styles—from ocean racing and the Royal Ocean Racing Club rule, from the narrow and deep Scandinavian racers, from open one designs; something from all the boats I had sailed went into her. I was delighted with the result—so delighted, in fact, that after several seasons of very competitive racing and happy cruising, I decided to build fiberglass versions of her for sale. Sigurd and I formed a company, Belle Ocean Racing. We called the design Norbelle, and the production was farmed out to Dalen Boats, a subsidiary of the tannery I was working for. We sold only ten, and learned that boatbuilding is a tough lot, but it was a great adventure and it produced my current fiberglass *Tresbelle*.

Then, in 1980, my son Gustave hatched the plan that eventually put *Tresbelle* and me here in mid-Atlantic headed across to Oslo. He was an officer in the Norwegian navy, and he arranged for the navy to charter *Tresbelle* from me (for a dollar), gave her the pseudonym *Nor-Am Friendship*, and entered her in the 1981 TwoStar. The TwoStar is a race from Plymouth, England, to Newport, Rhode Island. Crew is limited to two, and it is one of the toughest events around on boats and sailors both. Gustave and his fellow officer and friend Toffen-Thorleif Thorleifsson trained for a year, modified the hell out of my poor cruising boat, and then set off. They did well. They didn't win, not even in their class, but they beat more boats than beat them, and they proved to my satisfaction that a well-sailed monohull could do well against the speed-machine trimarans. She looked so old-fashioned coming into Newport with all of the multihulls from Class One and the other racing boats, but eighth out of thirty-two in Class Three (especially with a broken forestay for the last three-hundred miles of the race) made me very proud of both *Tresbelle* and her crew.

After the race, Gustave trusted me to take the boat home.

She was a salt-soaked mess, like any racing boat. Chris came aboard first. He's a Viking, by look and deed. Square through the shoulders and chest with no blockiness below, he might be coming over the bow of a longship instead of down the companionway. His red beard is better-trimmed, maybe, than Eric the Red's, but there is something about the clarity and calm in his pale gray eyes that lets you know almost at once that Chris is no wild man. He's the farthest thing from it. He's earned ever better wire-service jobs because of his careful reporting; he's restored a Brixham trawler from a hulk to a home; and nothing with parts and pawls to it is long a mystery to his mechanical inquirings. And he's a hell of a navigator and damn good man on deck.

Not all Scandianavian women are pretty and blond, but Tone is. There may have been some basis long ago for the lore that taking a woman to sea is bad luck, but it didn't come from women like her. Not from women who bake bread in a gale, stand their watches no matter what, have sense enough not to call attention to the obvious differences between girls and boys, and are wise and funny enough to be good companions anywhere.

From Newport we cleaned and tidied *Tresbelle* all the way to Boston. There, in the Coast Guard basin on Atlantic Avenue, we started the work of putting our beat-up boat back together. I had a big trunk full of cruising gear shipped to Boston. To lighten *Tresbelle*, Gustave had done without the table, pots and pans, and all of the other stuff that makes life at sea civilized. In addition to fixing the broken forestay and the roller-furling system that had to work with it, we replaced our intermediate shrouds, because they were starting to fray. The trunk arrived, the work was done, but Tone was still aloft taping cotter pins when the first of the guests arrived for our bon voyage party.

My partners from our international leather business in Worcester, Massachusetts, plus their families, some of my relatives, friends—we hadn't expected to fit all thirty-five below, but a cloudburst came out of the sticky July twilight, it must have been a hundred degrees, so we had no choice. Glimpses of navigator Chris in a sweltering blazer and tie, mastwoman Tone still in her jeans and cut-off T-shirt, good friends, champagne, and Ellen, the girl who more than anyone else got me through the pain of my marital separation . . . all fed my emotions. With fogged glasses and tears in my eyes, I toasted those we'd leave behind. From all corners of my little ship, including the four people wedged in the head, came back "Bon voyage."

Half drunk, dead tired, emotionally wrung dry, I still couldn't sleep. I must have cat-napped, but I can remember lying there, sweating, trying to trace each of the hundreds of sounds a boat makes, even tied at a dock.

Did I tie the boom down tight?

The fenders are squeaking. Are they riding up so we'll hit the pilings?

The little problems led on to bigger ones. The weather in

midocean. Would our food hold up? Would I hold up? And then on to Oslo, where I had worries too. I'd never sailed with Chris and Tone together. What kind of complications did it mean for me that they are ex-lovers? Normally being on an anchored or tied boat is very restful. The ship's sounds form a kind of cocoon and shut out the worries of the world. Now I felt as if we were already at sea. I watched and worried, I felt supertuned to every little squeak and clank, I couldn't get my body to go off watch.

Stiffly, creakily, I padded in my underwear to the companionway and went on deck. The cool breeze surprised me. The thundershower hadn't been just an isolated squall. The front stalled inland had finally come through. The breeze was strong, the stars were bright.

Why not get started?

Tresbelle could make a lot of miles with this nor'wester behind her. Why leave her tied here to the dock?

Why? The boat's a catastrophe, the crew's dog-tired . . . you're all wired up.

If you waste a fair breeze you deserve the doldrums.

More sailors' wisdom, but I needed to convince myself. I got dressed, straightened up, puttered around, stowed what I could, and cast off. Almost as soon as the engine was going Chris was on deck. No questions, not even a hello; he just turned to and helped me set the mainstall as we poked *Tresbelle*'s bow out into the inkiness of the harbor.

Ruby, emerald, diamond—the navigation flashers were pinpricking on and off all round. We got out from the marina lights and looked back at a dark skyline cut with swatches of light. Even at 0300 there were chunks and patches of light. STATE STREET BANK in grayish-blue capitals glowed up in the sky, again broken and distorted on the waves off to starboard. The pointed tower of the Old Custom House, decorous and spirelike among boxy skyscrapers, made me think grandiosely, "We're headed for the Old World."

To port were the purple and gold landing lights of Logan

Airport, white beacons and strobes that are "streetlights" along the left-hand side of the harbor channel. I felt happy and alive, cut free from land, beyond the dogwork of getting ready and already feeling the rhythms of sailing. Chris and I concentrated on finding unlit buoys and keeping clear of the flats just east of the airport.

Perched on one edge of it, the ocean seemed very big. We cut the engine and heard the hiss of our bow wave build as we surged down the dark fairway toward open water. Opposite the last lights of Logan was a small, medieval-looking set of ramparts—a castle? a fort?—with stone battlements, gun emplacements. In the aeroglow of the harsh airport lights it looked strange.

"My God," I said, pointing it out to Chris. "It's Oscarsborg."

Chris eyed the low stonework fort with its walls cut into scallops of white and black by the lights. Castle Island, South Boston, Massachusetts.

"If that's Oscarsborg, Bels, then I must have slept all the way across the ocean. Do you suppose we're already there?"

"There are stranger things in heaven and earth. Keep the dream in mind."

We set the jib.

With both sails drawing well, *Tresbelle* quickly cleared the outer channel, passed Boston Light scissoring the dark on her starboard hand, and sailed into the Atlantic.

Chapter Four

Oscarsborg is the harbor fort of Oslo. It sits on a low island in the channel leading up to the port from the Oslofjord. Ever since Viking times there has been fortification of some sort on the island. It is a sort of natural guardpost. In 1640, King Christian IV built a blockhouse on the half-mile rock, and succeeding generations have added improvements. King Oscar I commissioned the present low stone ramparts, and they were finished in 1855. The last time the fort was modernized was in 1893. The long-necked eleven-inch guns put in position then were so awesome that they inspired Biblical nicknames: Moses, Joshua, and Aaron.

By April 9, 1940, there was quite a bit more to the fortification than the long-barreled cannon: there were shore batteries of smaller but more modern pieces, there was a submerged breakwater that narrowed the channel and forced ships to come close alongside Oscarsborg, and there was a torpedo battery hidden in the rocks. Top-secret but untested, it was manned, like the fort itself, mostly by school-age young men who had been in training less than five weeks.

The garrison was on alert. The day before, the British had laid mines in Norwegian waters. Ever since the British had pierced Norway's neutrality to board the German ship *Altmark* in the Jøssingfjord, things had been edgy. Commander Eriksen had no idea what he and his men might face as a result of international developments.

Aboard the Royal Norwegian Navy patrol vessel *Pol III*, skipper Leif Welding Olsen was almost ready to turn and head for home. Since sunset he had been working his creaky 111-foot steam-driven ex-whaler (launched in 1926) south down the seventy-mile Oslofjord toward the sea. Now it was close to midnight, time to turn and make north for base. The fog was thick in places, thick enough to make surveillance of shipping difficult.

An older design, *Pol III* had noticeably less hull above the waterline than modern ships her size. Welding Olsen, though, was elevated well above the deck in his two-story "fire-tower" bridge right forward of her steamstack. On the bow was a single 76mm cannon. Aboard with Welding Olsen were fourteen sailors. Norway's governments, most recently socialist, had a long tradition of pacifism. Under their "broken rifle" credo the country had avoided war for more than a century.

But war had recently intruded into Norway. The *Altmark*, one of the supply ships for the battleship *Admiral Graf von Spee*, had fled the British task force that sank the Nazi battleship and had taken refuge in the Jossingfjord in February. The Norwegian navy searched her, and she was allowed sanctuary. HMS *Cossack*, a British destroyer, then forced her way into the fjord, seized *Altmark*, and liberated the more than four hundred Allied prisoners who had been hidden in her hold. There followed a crossfire of accusations and pronouncements. Guarding Norway's coast was getting tougher.

Pol III had been patrolling the western shore of the fjord.

Welding Olsen headed out toward the ship channel, angling north as he went. There were lookouts in the crow's nest, on the bow, and beside him on the bridge, but Welding Olsen saw the ship first. The fog was spotty. Looking down a lane between two fogbanks, he saw a large, cottony bow wave—no lights, just a bow wave as high as his bridge—and a dark shape behind it three or four times higher than that. Against the loom of the lights of the far shore he made out the pyramid silhouette of a huge warship.

He called for full power and turned to parallel the intruder's course. She was making at least twice his speed. He held off signaling until she got close enough to reach with his spotlight. Before the return glare of four big searchlights blinded him, Captain Welding Olsen saw that he'd encountered a battleship, or at least a cruiser. No navigation lights, no signal lights, just a steaming shape making twenty knots through Norwegian waters.

Welding Olsen's signalman flashed out dash-dot-dash, code meaning "I wish to communicate with you."

Blackness. No response.

The signalman flashed dash-dot-dot-dash, "Stop carrying out your intentions. Watch for my signal."

The warship was abeam of *Pol III*. She had not signaled or slowed down.

"Send L," ordered Welding Olsen. Dot-dash-dot-dot, "Stop your vessel instantly."

Still the warship steamed ahead. She made no signal in return, but the men of *Pol III* could hear the distant whooping of sirens as she summoned her men to battle stations.

"Prepare to fire a warning shot. Aim high and ahead of him. Fire when ready."

Flame shot from the muzzle of the bow cannon. The tracer shell arced ahead of the ship and burst overhead fifty meters off the water. The hum from her engines and slosh of waves as she rolled past drowned out the clacking from the signalman's light. Still no reply, but the warship's searchlights swiveled aft to hold *Pol III* in a pool of glare.

"Warship astern, sir. A point off our port quarter."

The passing ship paid no attention to the warning shot. Astern came an equally large warship, also unlit. It too fixed *Pol III* in the unfriendly glare of four huge spotlights. With deliberate calm, Captain Welding Olsen shouted over the claxoning sirens and the clank and throb of his stressed steam engine, "Red signals. Fire two. Fire two. Fire them *now*."

The signalman took a moment. Two Roman-candle-like red flares, the signal that hostile ships were in Nowegian waters, popped high into the fog above.

There was more movement. Before the flares even disappeared into the overhanging cloud, the bridge lookout reported, "Ships, more ships a point off the starboard quarter." Skittering into his vision the skipper saw the pulses of spray and changing silhouettes of small boats moving very fast.

"Hard right rudder!" he shouted. "Torpedo boats," he mumbled to himself.

Welding Olsen waited for *Pol III* to begin her turn. She continued straight.

"Right full rudder. Got that?" He listened to his voice tube. No reply from the helmsman and no change of course.

Louder: "Rudder hard over to starboard."

The helmsman, a level below, evidently could not make out his orders. There was too much noise for him to hear through the voice tubes. Welding Olsen hated to go to the steering station to command, because the helmsman had only his small helming port to see from. Still . . .

He had started below when he saw a broom on the deck of the bridge. Holding it by the bristles, he leaned over the forward edge of the bridge and down in front of the helmsman and made hard motions to the right.

No response.

He tried again.

In a moment he felt the ship list as the rudder went over and *Pol III* began her turn to starboard.

Pol III's bow cannon couldn't get a good shot at the torpedo boats approaching from astern. Now she was spinning through a gradual arc to put them on her bow. The warships continued on. Their searchlights and sirens were gone. He tried his voice tube.

"Steady there."

Pol III steadied on her course, right at the oncoming boats. They opened up with machine guns as the range narrowed. Then an explosion came back aft. A fire started amidships along the starboard rail.

"Check the damage aft," he told his exec. "Steady there, hold on. Keep her power on." *Pol III* was hardly maneuverable with her slow-spinning single screw, shallow rudder, and deep hull. She was pointed now on a collision course with the closest torpedo boat. She cranked off a single shot with her bow cannon, and it appeared to connect. Welding Olsen pressed ahead. Maintaining as much speed as he could, he aimed his burning, listing boat for the nearest German. Bow to bow they closed until the torpedo boat turned quickly to port. He had waited too long, and *Pol III* rammed him just aft of his wheelhouse.

Pol III rolled up and nearly over the gunboat. Decks broke and splintered under her heavy bow. There was surprisingly little impact, because the torpedo boat rolled almost underneath her. The Germans must have been stunned and thrown around. Their guns were silent, their boat's engines uncontrolled.

Welding Olsen was wounded. By the time his crew had gotten him down from the bridge, the fire to starboard was fierce, the list to starboard had gotten worse, and a circle of torpedo boats was closing on them. The crew abandoned ship. In the melee boarding the ship's pram, Welding Olsen was lost into the water. He was too weak to hold a line and disappeared. The German torpedo boat, *Albatros*, was holed but stayed afloat.

Pol III's crew was picked up and imprisoned by the Nazis. *Pol III*, burned-out, blunt-bowed, and lifeless, was towed to Tönsberg the next day, where she was taken over by the Kriegsmarine and repaired. She spent the war as a Nazi patrol vessel. After the war she returned to Norwegian hands and was a freighter. She has now been fitted with a live well and is still in service today. Renamed *Fisktrans*, she is transporting fish, for fish farmers.

Captain Lief Welding Olsen was the first Norwegian to die in the still-to-be-declared war against the Third Reich.

Through the fog and far away, *Pol III*'s signal flares have been seen. By 0300, Commander Eriksen knows that hostile ships are steaming toward Oslo. As they close with the coast near Filtvet, they are identified. The lead ship is the new battle cruiser *Blücher*. Astern of her are the older, smaller heavy cruisers *Emden* and *Lützow*. Gunboats, torpedo boats, and a pair of destroyers nestle in behind the big guns and heavy armor of the leaders.

By 0330 the ships are in sight in the weak glow of the false dawn.

"They meant to be here earlier, in the dark," Eriksen says to his gunnery officer.

Blücher steams on at speed. The rest of the flotilla slows down.

"They want the leader to have room to maneuver in the strait," Eriksen thinks aloud.

The tall light-gray ship, the black rocks still half covered with wet snow, bare in spots, the growing glow as the water reflects the lightening sky. It is 0400.

Around the guns it is quiet. In the bunkers, in the towers and the tunnels of Oscarsborg, it is quiet. *Blücher* makes no noise as she cuts across the sound toward the strait.

"Range three thousand meters."

Eriksen nods.

Blücher's exhaust plumes up and to starboard in the gentle westerly breeze.

"Range twenty-five hundred meters."

"These guns are so slow, and Joshua's not firing . . . we'll only have the two shots. I just hope she comes closer," Eriksen says. "She must be trying to sneak through. Why is she going so slow? Wouldn't you start to shell us from there?"

Blücher, beamy, tall, her portholed hull flared cobralike at the bow, dipping low to the water amidships, steams at six knots toward the strait.

"Range two thousand meters."

"If only she comes closer before she shoots. Hold on."

"Range fifteen hundred meters."

From Oscarsborg you can see the sailors on *Blücher*'s fantail, the open mouths of her twelve-inch guns.

"Not yet. Hang on. Keep coming, please, you beast. We may have broken the rifle, but we fixed it for you."

"Range one thousand meters."

"Yes," says Eriksen. "Yes. Hit them!"

The strangely muted discharge of long-barreled Moses, the clang and complaint of the recoil mechanism, the gasps, and then the cheers. The antiaircraft battery aboard *Blücher* is geysering steam, there are red-yellow flashes, blackening smoke, spreading flames.

Another *whomp*, this time from Aaron. The spotting aircraft spins like a pinwheel. Blue-gray smoke followed by fire. A second explosion, and flames fan to either side of the stern deck. More cheers. From shore the puffs of the batteries, the sound of distant concussions, the chaos from more hits aboard *Blücher*. Smoke bearding her bridge, flames crackling over her incredible length, she drifts sideways, pushed by wind and tide toward the channel mouth.

Burbles at the waterline, bubbles of oil in the water, a list developing to port. The torpedoes! Spits of flame dart out her hull ports, hose jets turn to steam. She's in the channel now, helpless and burning, listing more to port every minute, water lapping the edge of her deck, boats dropping, splashing, overturning, tangling on her high side. Heads dotting the water, drifting patches of flame.

It is 0622. Bow submerged, *Blücher* rolls to port, turns bottom up, and in an accelerating glide pocked by hisses and small explosions, slides forward and down. Her props and rudder lift momentarily high above the water, and she sinks.

Chapter Five

scarsborg was about fifteen miles from our apartment in Oslo. We went there for picnics sometimes; I sailed by it when I was a kid. I'd finished my homework. I wanted to stay up, but my parents waved me off to bed. My parents and my older sister Sylvei were still talking excitedly. April 8, 1940. That morning the British had laid mines. No one knew what would happen. The guesses were wild. If we have a war, I thought to myself, maybe we won't have any school.

We were all asleep when the sirens went off. It was quite a shock. The wail seemed to be inside the house. Then there was the racheting ak-ak of the antiaircraft guns and the piercing whine of the dive-bombers. And I heard bombs going off.

I sat up in bed. At first I was just overcome by the noise. Then I realized that it was an air raid. But I had no idea what to do. I felt penned inside my bedroom. I sat up. Then I began to shake. The covers around me, my eyes and ears still struggling to orient me, I began to shake. Tremors, uncontrollable spasms. I don't remember being terribly scared, but I was acting like a mouse mesmerized by a rattlesnake, a rattlesnake with very loud rattles.

My father rushed in, shouted instructions, and ran out again. We were leaving the house. We had to get dressed. "It's cold out there, and damp. Hurry." We race down the stairs. I was better now. Once I had something to do I stopped shaking. I stumbled out behind the rest of the family. My little sister Kirsten was wrapped in a coat bigger than she was. Sylvei seemed unsure of what was happening but thoroughly annoyed by all this. Mother, calm and clucking, was still the family center.

"Where are we going?" we asked.

"To the park. It will be safer in the park. When they bomb we'll be better off in the park than close to the houses," my father said.

Vigeland Park was a short walk away, on a ridge, and there, where the houses thinned out, we could see the city below. There were fires on the waterfront, but it looked as though the houses hadn't been torched. There were sirens still, and planes overhead.

"That's a swastika! It's the Germans," I said as a fighter-bomber flew past. "It's the Germans, not the Russians," I said to Kirsten. "I thought the Russians were attacking us as they attacked Finland."

Planes passed overhead in the dawn light, some quite low. Out over the city the air was full of planes. We didn't see bombs, though.

Whinggg! A bullet ricocheted off the rocks behind us. A plane was already pulling up to turn. I wondered why they would strafe individuals, women and children. I wondered if there were more fighters lurking around the park. I wondered why we were standing vulnerable and sheepish out in the open.

"Come on!" we shouted and ran for the trees. Kirsten was just ahead of me. She slipped. I helped her up on the run and

we made it to the limited shelter of the woods at the edge of
the park. I felt better now that I wasn't a quivering mass, now
I had done something halfway usual.

What the hell were we doing here? Why on earth should
we be sliding around in the mud in the fog at dawn? A Mes-
serschmitt thundered over the park while we stood at the edge
of the trees. What ever the rules, women or children or whatever, there wasn't any doubt that it would be wise to stay out
of sight until this whole thing settled down.

We caught our breaths and stood there. "What is going to
happen to us? Are the Germans coming to kill us? Why? What
did we ever do to Germany?" Father stood befuddled but defiant.
A championship marksman, he had never fired a weapon in
anger. Instead of holding a rifle he stood in the mud with his
family. Mother stood close to him, gripping his arm. Kirsten
watched wide-eyed and nuzzled close to Mother. Sylvei, scared,
angry, wanting to do something, huddled with me.

"You know," I said, "I thought it was the Russians. Until I
saw the swastikas. I thought it was the Russians coming at
last."

"I thought it was the British, with all of their mines and
everything," Sylvei said.

Standing at the edge of the woods, we felt cold and foolish.
The houses weren't being bombed. There were no other families in the park. It seemed the Luftwaffe was strafing and buzzing
targets but not dropping bombs. Maybe the Germans knew
already that they were in control. Maybe there was nothing
left to bomb. Maybe we were the only targets left for the whole
Luftwaffe. We had a brief family conference; no one wanted
to stay in the park! Father led us back to our flat.

The rest of the morning we filled sandbags—to protect us
from fires, from bombs—and listened to the radio. We learned
Nazi paratroops had tried to arrest the king. We heard about
the sinking of *Blücher*. Most of the twenty-five hundred men
aboard had been killed. We learned that the king had escaped.

He declared war from Elverum, in eastern Norway. Imagine, our three and a half million declaring war on the Reich. But still it made us feel much better.

Norway Radio went off the air; there were new voices. In both Norwegian and German, they told us: "Soldiers, sailors, and airmen of the Fatherland today bring to Norway a new era of brotherhood and cooperation. The British meddlers have been expelled, the links have been forged for a glorious new order." The Nazis were proclaiming their arrival.

"Mother, do we have to keep filling sandbags?"

"Kirsten dear, please."

"Mother, what good will sandbags do?"

"Arne, please, it is better to be safe."

"I'm becoming a sand crab and the city of Oslo's being invaded. We ought to get out and see what's happening."

"Sylvei, dear, you're safer here at home. Keep digging."

Vidkun Quisling came on the radio next. For years he had headed Norway's tiny Fascist Party. He'd run in every conceivable election, and never won a thing. Now, on the heels of the Nazis, he addressed the nation: "The glory of this day is matched only by the brightness of Norway's future. Today the help of our brother country Germany has enabled us to throw off the decadent and outmoded monarchy. The king has fled. The king no longer rules in Norway.

"As your new prime minister I will assure that the bonds between the Reich and Norway grow tighter and stronger. We will work together to fulfill this country's destiny as leader among the northern peoples and pillar of the Aryan League." And on and on.

It was an important speech. Had it made any sense, had the rhetoric cut into our confusion and enlightened us, it might have built some following. Delivered in Fascist clichés by a weak-chinned loser to justify his own arrogant and small-minded grab for power, it showed absolutely no gift for leadership, no ability to inspire. It made it very easy for most Norwegians. If collaboration with the Nazis meant accepting Quisling, we would resist, we would all resist. Quisling's first speech to the nation was all that we needed to be unified, the country against him and against the Nazis.

There was so much happening in Oslo that mother wouldn't let any of us leave the house. The next day the news was everywhere: "The British are coming. The RAF will bomb the Germans out of the city." The rumor flew from one neighborhood to another.

At last we had something to do. Along with some 300,000 others, we took to the streets and evacuated Oslo. Buses were jam-packed, trolleys shuttled back and forth with people and belongings; there was a sea of bicycles and a human tide of people on foot. Sylvei's boyfriend, I remember, transported Mother on the back of his Harley-Davidson.

We didn't go too far—about two hours' walk across the city to my aunt's house. She lived just outside Oslo on the coast. I don't suppose our evacuation would have made us much safer if the RAF commenced bombing, but that event never came. At least ten times I heard the "high-pitched whine of British bomber engines" that I'd read about, but it was always between my ears. The air raids never really materialized. Sheepishly, individually, the throng that had flocked to the country filtered back slowly to Oslo over the next two weeks. A heroic mass movement out and back—it accomplished absolutely nothing, but it still seems to me an indication of how completely the Germans turned us upside down with their invasion.

When we got home we found Germans everywhere, garrisoned in the schools, bivouacked in the parks, posted outside downtown buildings, riding the transport, manning checkpoints along the streets, monopolizing all of the best restaurants and cafés, and establishing themselves in the downtown stores and offices. There were big white posters everywhere, white with large block letters in black proclaiming, "SKUTT BLIR

DEN SOM:"—Shot will be the one who:—and there followed a listing.

   —gives information to the enemy
   —conceals arms
   —fails to show respect for the Reich
   —joins an illegal organization

Dark to us was the look of our future.

Chapter Six

Just a bit of superstructure showing, a ship came into view. It was more likely to be a freighter than a tanker, but I couldn't tell for sure.

"Should I try her on the radio, maybe get some weather?" asked Chris.

"Freighter, unidentified freighter, freighter heading eastward, this is the sailboat on your bow. Come in."

It's an awkward way to make contact, but sometimes it works eventually:

"Sailboat *Tray bella aqui* cargo *Reggio Calabria*."

The freighter gave us her position so that we could check our own fix against it. Then she told us something about the weather. The Azores High was parked halfway between Bermuda and the Azores. It had intensified and broadened, and it sat right in the middle of where we were going. From Boston to Land's End, England, was our route, and across that course the freighter reported a big parking lot of totally flat calm.

"Non c'e multo vento"—Not much wind.

Three full days at sea and we'd made over four hundred miles—425 at noon. But if we got into the high and were becalmed, there was no telling how long we'd be stuck. To keep in good air the best bet looked to be to stay in the westerly flow around the high. To do that meant heading farther north, which meant cutting across the Grand Banks. The probability of fog and the certainty of wall-to-wall fishing boats made that not such a happy course either.

"I think we must have wind," Tone said. "It can be foggy anyplace, but if we're going to cross we need wind."

"Have you taken to writing notices to mariners in your sea-wise old age, Tone, my love? We probably won't get many sun sights on the Banks," said Chris, "But that doesn't bother me if it doesn't bother you."

"We have enough diesel to motor for forty hours. We could power through some of the worst of the calm," I told them.

"Yes," Tone said, "but, we have to have power for our land-fall, and for emergencies. I think we must have wind. We must go north."

"What does that do to our course for Land's End?" asked Chris. "It sure makes it a longer way around."

"Well," Tone said, "why do we have to go south around England? We can go north around Ireland and Scotland. The Shetlands are beautiful, and the English Channel is full of car ferries—almost as crowded as the Grand Banks."

"You know, I was thinking that if we went that way . . . I've always wanted to go through the Caledonian Canal."

"You mean through Scotland?" said Chris.

"You go right through the lochs. Yes. Loch Ness . . . hunting the monster? The country's beautiful. And it's a shorter way, really."

And so we went north.

"Arne, can you come up?"

It is early morning. I am making breakfast. Tone is alone on deck. We have begun standing two-man watches, one to steer and one as lookout, now that we're in the fog, but I've snuck down into the galley.

"There's some traffic around us. Can you come up and figure this out?"

I come right up. Chris, too, rolls out of his quarterberth even though he should be sleeping.

"I hear his bow wave," Tone says as she points off our starboard bow into the murk. I can see only about two boat lengths ahead of the bow.

"I think he's about there, off our starboard bow. I've heard his bow wave for a couple of minutes. I can't hear anything else, though . . . no horn, no engines. But the wave sounds like he's pushing a lot of water."

Chris comes on deck, motions with the foghorn. I nod, and he gives a long blast.

"Do you think they'll hear that on the bridge of a tanker?" Tone asks.

I hear the bow wave now, too . . . deceiving in the fog, but I imagine it's a big trawler or a small lighter or tanker pushing that water toward us. We have our radar reflector at the spreader. We hope that they can see us, but you can't just sit there.

"Try them on the radio, Chris."

I hear the wave, but Tone was right—no engines, no horns or bells, no throb from the prop. "Maybe it's not a trawler."

"I can't get anyone."

"No one answers the damn phone!" says Tone.

"Would you like to try placing a few calls, Miss Lonely-hearts?"

"Not now, Chris," she answers.

The bow wave still sounds the same. It could be coming right at us. I check the engine controls. Ignition key in place; we are ready.

"Try more blasts."

We give our "one long blast" (sailboat on starboard tack) signal four or five times. No answer at all. Still, the wave sound is right on our bow. Is it standing still? The boat makes some noise as she moves along, but the fog around us seems like a silent room, a room where we're walled in with the eerie cresting sound of nearby waves, a silence that lets us hear only that mystery sound and nothing more.

"Do you think it's a fishboat hove to and washing his deck?" Chris wonders aloud as we ghost through the dripping grayness.

"You know, it might just be fish."

Chris and Tone look at me blankly.

"Let's see. Sharpen up and head for the sound."

Tone comes up; we trim for the new heading and wait. *Tresbelle* makes her own sounds as she schusses through the flat gray water and the luminous fog, but there's no missing the pop-pop-pop-pop of ripples slapping together out there where we can't see.

Whatever it is, its bearing stays constant. It gets louder as we close with it. The rippling sound out there has us skewered. It can't be a ship. It's not moving much at all.

Tone is steering, I'm on the bow. Chris keeps sounding the horn at shorter and shorter intervals. *Tresbelle*'s decks are wet with the mist. The low sun through the morning fog cuts our vision further, the way headlights turn mist into a gauzy curtain. I sign to Tone to come more to starboard . . . that's good . . . a louder wave-rush, and then we are there. The slate-colored water dimples and becomes a black overfalls. The sound of criss-crossing wavelets is a *pok-a, pok-a* plashing like lots of hands slapping the surface of a swimming pool, like a spring brook rushing between rocks.

Fish! It's fish . . . fish roiling the surface in a feeding orgy. They're snapping and chasing right below the surface. Sprays and droplets shoot up where they're breaking the surface. It's loud enough so we have to shout together in the cockpit. I see silver flashes beneath the cut-up surface where big ones roll and dart. "What kind are they?" Tone asks.

"I don't know, but I'll get the lines."

They were pollock. Without altering course we caught enough for a supper. With a dip net Chris brought aboard a bucketful of the bait they were chasing—baby octopi. Pollock stuffed with octopi: I was ready for a mid-ocean feast.

The rest of the day was tense. There was more hidden in the fog than bountiful gifts of loaves and pollock. We heard horns, engines, the clanking of deck gear. We weaved our way through the fishing fleet, spotting maybe one in three as the fog thinned enough to give us perhaps a quarter-mile circle of visibility. About 1600 we were concentrating on the sound of engines approaching astern when *Wham* . . . out of the fog one hundred yards to starboard we saw a huge steel bow. It was a Russian trawler; the hammer and sickle were prominent embossed above her stem. Luckily she was moving slowly, maybe three knots, because she was zeroed right at us. We crossed a bit more than one hundred yards in front of her. If she'd been steaming instead of dragging a trawl we might have been run down before we could do anything. She continued to come, seemingly oblivious to us. Powering in a cross-swell with no stability from speed, she wallowed in painful-looking cycles, coming close to dipping the ends of her protruding net poles at the end of each roll.

Toward evening I was down below plotting a sauce for the pollock, dicing octopi, and sautéing onions. Usually I like to heave to for a festive meal, but here on the Banks that didn't seem like such a good idea. So, damp and chill as it was on deck, we bundled up for dinner so that we could all eat together in the cockpit. The long daylight of late July was a help, and the Mersault that Ellen had given the ship at our bon voyage party went very well. Pollock stuffed with a mixture of the diced octopi, onions, garlic, and celery sautéed together in olive oil and mixed with some crumbs from our bread locker, fish fresh enough so we could still hear it slapping, gift fish from the sea as regal as I've ever eaten, served with the last of our garden peas, mashed potatoes, and crème caramel, brought a life to *Tresbelle*'s cold damp cockpit that made our day of ducking and dodging across the Banks seem almost worth it.

The breeze dropped, the fog eased up, and it was so pleasant watching the light change as the sun buried itself in the fog blanket that none of us wanted to go below after dinner.

"I'll be happy if we never have another day like this one, though," said Chris, sipping his coffee. "I never knew that it was so crowded out here."

"Maybe if we had radar and a working loran C and a big diesel with lots of fuel we'd be happier," Tone said.

"Well, so far we've had wind," I offered.

"Bels, stop trying to justify yourself. We think the Grand Banks is a lovely spot," Tone answered.

"Besides," I said, "after a few days of slatting around down there to the south with no wind and full-time sun we'd be attacking each other with winch handles."

"Seriously, Bels, doesn't this worry you? I mean, all of this traffic makes it dangerous."

"True, that was a close call this afternoon, but you can have close calls in a car. They don't stop you from driving."

"No," Chris contributed, "but you sort of have to drive. We don't really have to be out here. Well, come to think of it, I'm not so sure of that."

"Sorry?"

"I guess that doesn't make much sense. What I mean is, I think I would let them take my car keys away before I'd let them ban voyaging. Well, pretty fanciful, but you know what I mean. Cars are necessities. We don't have to be this crazy, to be out here looking for trouble."

"Well," Tone said, "I can tell you fresh pollock stuffed with octopi is even better than it sounds, especially when it takes so little trouble to catch it. We certainly got something out of toady besides trouble."

"It was good, wasn't it?"

"You know, Bels," she continued, "you never talk very much about the camps and what you went through. We hear you yelling sometimes in your dreams. It's so beautiful now, I don't want to spoil it, but . . . we don't have any bow waves bothering us."

I started to say something, but she kept on. "I mean, today, when we thought we heard a bow wave, you took us right in there to find out what it was. If it had been up to me I think I would have stayed the hell away."

"If it was up to you we'd have had corned beef hash for dinner," sniped Chris.

"The camps were certainly . . . hard. Hard to survive, hard to understand, hard to get over. Maybe all I really got from the camps was a sense that . . . of how sweet life is. It's certainly not new or profound or anything. Anytime your life is threatened you appreciate life more. I guess it's that simple. That's what the death camps gave me . . . life. I guess I don't talk more than I do because what I say sounds so foolish to me."

"I'm sorry, Bels," said Tone.

"No, I'm sorry. I was just thinking. Thinking about what you said. I don't know what to say about the camps, exactly, but I do know that a walking scarecrow like me would have walked around the world for a meal like ours tonight back in the days of the camps."

"Does that have anything to do with us taking the long way home, Bels?"

"Shut up, Chris, let the man talk," Tone said.

"There is a friend of mine, Tore Hytten, we were together in Natzweiler and Dachau. To this day he still keeps tins of meat under his bed. I'm almost the same way. I get nervous and erratic if I know there's no meal in sight. And I get happier and happier the more I can cook for my friends. You've seen the pictures. When we were released we were truly skin and bone. No buttocks, no calves, no thighs . . . no flesh and hardly any muscle. It was all gone. At my lowest I weighed ninety pounds. When you consider that I'm six feet two, that's *thin*. . . ."

For a while my friend Ragnvald and I used to eat coffee grounds. Well, they were actually the grounds from the coffee surrogate they gave us. No nutritional value at all, but they gave us the feeling we'd eaten something. The standard concentration camp diet began with a bowl of coffee surrogate at five in the morning. Some people were able to save the one piece of bread given out in the evening and have it with the coffee. Theories varied about whether you should eat your bread when you got it or save half for the morning. Some of the guys broke their bread into many small pieces and had a piece every hour. I had my lovely piece of lovely bread all together, in one go . . . finished and done with. I promised myself that at the end of the war I'd buy that heavy dark rye bread—I have no idea what it was made of—and eat it a loaf at a time.

The great event of the day was the noon meal. We had one pint of soup, which was made of water and cabbage, and probably one pound of meat for a hundred people. Sometimes they put in potatoes. Ragnvald and I were very good at getting to the garbage first so that we came away with potato peelings to eat.

Each prisoner had a spoon—mostly wooden spoons. We had metal bowls. When lunch call came we lined up in single file and the soup was brought from the kitchen in large aluminum containers. Sometimes you got mostly water in your bowl; if you were luckier you got the thick stuff. The trick was to position yourself in the line so that you could be served when the container was almost empty . . . the good, thick stuff sank to the bottom.

Oh, how this little ceremony occupied us. We played it like million-dollar lottery. If you were too smart you could lose ut completely because when you got your turn to be served ere would be nothing left. In Natzweiler one of the prisners, a Russian, managed somehow to steal a container of e lunchtime soup. He was found dead after drinking someing like ten quarts on his own.

On Sundays we sometimes had macaroni soup. I can still avor the memory of it. If you were to go down the galley and ring some up here, I'd probably throw it overboard, but then was something to dream about.

Your body has ways of dealing with hunger. As your stomch shrinks you feel it less. Nonetheless, we felt it. There were iffering ideas on how we should deal with it mentally. One roup said that you must never think, speak, or dream about od. I belonged to the other group. We composed menus ncessantly, spoke of food constantly, shared and elaborated pon food fantasies. It must have been tough on the other roup to listen to us. My dream was at least four helpings of eat pudding, green peas, boiled potatoes, and thick brown ravy.

When you have dysentery you become dehydrated. I have en people dwindle away, collapse, and die in a matter of ours from dehydration. I remember the thirst that I had during one of my dysentery attacks. I was ready to give my right and for a bottle of pilsner beer. Meat pie and pilsner beer . . simple as that.

The urge for eggs and bacon was also worth talking about. Vhen I got home I got up at two o'clock every morning and ade myself eggs, bacon, and home fries and ate it all, withut second thought or interruption.

Ragnvald and I, knowing full well that NN—*Nacht und Nebel*—prisoners would never get to be *die Prominenten*, big hots, and get to work in the kitchen, became scavengers. In e fields, the garbage, around the camp, anywhere where there ight be something edible, there we would be. Many kept

their bread rations in sacks around their necks. They were ofte
robbed. And there were times when the liver was cut out of
dead prisoner and eaten. Hunger plays with your mind, and
am proud to say that the Norwegians held together to figh
against it. It was rare that Norwegian stole from Norwegia
. . . there were only isolated cases, and in every one the thie
had given up. Usually they died not long after.

"Give me some more coffee, will you, Chris? This maudli
stuff makes me thirsty . . . hungry, too."

"Bels, I didn't know all of that. It makes me want to fill m
pockets with chocolate bars," Tone said.

Taking the coffeepot from its wedged-in spot in a corner c
the cockpit, Chris poured my cup full. "It's funny, after thi
morning's riches from the sea—pretty easy to harvest—

"I'll clean up the galley and take the watch with the Hershe
Queen."

I didn't dream of meat pies or fish jumping into the boa
but I slept. At midnight I was a bit bleary joining the other tw
in the cockpit, and it didn't register with any particular urgenc
when Tone said, "We've been hearing engines astern for
while now. Fog has come back in a bit. Breeze is about wha
it was, maybe a bit lighter. Until we heard those engines I wa
thinking this was like being in one of the mountain valleys i
the winter . . . alone with whiteness all around."

I was still slapping myself awake, still fixed on our alone
ness, when another part of my mind said: No, we aren't alon
out here.

We saw the grainy flashes of a searchlight first. Before lon
a towering shape broke the mist curtain astern. I thought
was a fishing boat, and as it overtook us quickly about tw
hundred yards off to port I could see that it was indeed, a b
trawler. I saw a few figures on deck; it was doing maybe thre
times our speed. To my surprise, she throttled down. Wit
her big engines just ticking over she kept pace with us as w

sailed through the light air and fog. I lighted up the sails with
our flashlight. We heard voices across the eight boat lengths
of water that separated us.

I went below and tried to raise the ship on the radio. "Trawler, unidentified trawler, trawler close abeam of sailboat *Tresbelle*, come in."

No luck.

"He must have seen us," said Chris. "I've been shining the
light on the sail ever since we heard him."

It was hard to believe. The three of us saw what was happening, but we couldn't believe it. We were still and staring,
the three of us all seated in the cockpit. We heard a roar, we
saw the lights swing, we even saw her stern hunker deeper into
the water as her engine revved higher. Waves churned under
the trawler's counter and, she started ahead, and gathering speed
she turned under full power to aim right at us.

Despite the dark and the shreds of fog, the image was clear.
I saw both running lights, two white steaming lights in line,
one above the other, lined up and pointing square at me. High,
rounded bow, anchors tucked up on either side, and a dark
row of wheelhouse windows seemingly vacant. Fifty yards away,
the boat was coming for us. It was like being trapped in a car
stuck on a railroad crossing, like standing in the middle of an
alley with a truck speeding at you.

I turned the ignition key and applied the power all at the
same time. I pushed the engine into gear as soon as it caught.
Chris had the wheel, Tone the light, and we could only watch
and wait.

Tresbelle seemed agonizingly slow to accelerate, but we picked
up way enough to surge forward and cross the trawler's bow by
no more than two boat lengths.

Scared, shaken, angry we watched the trawler lights. They
continued straight on out into the fog, softened, and disappeared.

Did Tone really hear laughter as the trawler went by? What
the bloody hell?

Chapter Seven

Overlooking the fjord and the coast road, my aunt's house was a fine perch for observing the arrival of the Nazis. We spent two weeks there after "Evacuation Day," that day after the invasion when everyone fled the city. While we were there I used to watch the soldiers marching, the troop ships unloading, and the transport planes coming in to the airport. It was like watching a parade or like playing with toy soldiers. I was fifteen, and the war was great sport to me. Far off, out there, on the edge of real life, I watched the war machine roll in. It was soundless, bloodless, and virtually painless. I was much happier and more excited now than I had been going to school.

The Weserübung, or Weser Operation, was named for a river that flows into the North Sea. It was the Nazis' invasion, a series of well-planned and swiftly played chess moves, a "war game," a strategic exercise that had a kind of textbook perfection. If Hitler had been bloodied earlier, he might not have pressed so far, but Weserubung must have made him more confident in the power of his machine and the cleverness with which he could use it.

The Germans took troop ships and disguised them as freighters. Poised offshore, sometimes even tied up inside the ports, these "Trojan ships" landed in cities like Trondheim, Stavanger, Kristiansand, and Bergen and off-loaded their troops, and the towns were taken with hardly a skirmish.

In another well-coordinated strike, Hitler sent *Blücher* and her flotilla to train their assemblage of heavy guns on Oslo and demand capitulation while putting marines ashore to capture the king and the members of his government. Had not *Pol III* and the guns of Oscarsborg foiled that armored attempt to force the strait at Drøbak Sound, the king might never have gotten away to form a legitimate government in London. Even though the flotilla behind *Blücher* turned tail and never forced the strait at Oscarsborg, we were still so poorly prepared, so unready to even think about war, that the Nazis captured Oslo with less than a thousand men.

Our few antiaircraft batteries did a good job, and some Luftwaffe planes were shot down, but our guns ran out of ammunition before long and the Nazis had total control of the air. Nine Gloucester Gladiator biplanes, the entire fighter power of Norway, threw themselves at the ME-109s, but they were all shot down within minutes. Strafing and very light bombing were enough to keep us terrified and disorganized. The Germans took the airport—against only minimal resistance—and then brought in transport planes full of troops. The airlifted troops joined the paratroops in taking the government buildings and the radio station. The better part of the invasion was over.

The king escaped with the government ministers, though. They declared war on Germany, ordered a general mobilization of all men, and fought on from the unoccupied parts of Norway. French alpine troops, Polish volunteers, and a British division were landed within two to three weeks to help. Given the superior numbers (at least twenty to one) that the Wehrmacht enjoyed and the fact that air cover for the Norwegian forces was nonexistent, it's amazing we were able to retake Narvik, far in the north, and to hold out as long as we did. Finally, to avoid what certainly would have been a massacre, the king declared an armistice on June 7, 1940. He and his ministers boarded the British cruiser *Devonshire* and were evacuated. They then set up a government in exile in London that became the focus of free Norwegian efforts from then on. But Norway, a free country since 1814 and one that had lived in peace for over a century, was now completely controlled by the forces of the Third Reich.

While we were camped out at my aunt's house, the invaders seemed remote and unreal. I watched the Nazis marching the coast road from the house we'd visited ever since I could remember. The Nazis seemed an exciting distraction, but I was certain "real life" was just around the corner somehow.

At last we went home. In downtown Oslo, the Nazis were much harder to ignore. My old playground, Vestkantorvet near Vigeland Park, was the staging area for their tanks. I had never seen a real tank, certainly not at close range. It was good to meet up with Jon again after the evacuation and all that time with my sisters. The first thing we did was go down to the park for a proper look at the panzers. There was a rope between the street and the play area where they had the tanks. A young soldier, maybe nineteen or twenty, was guarding the rope. A handful of kids were there. He was talking to them in the simplest German.

"*Wir sind ja gute Freunde.*" We are good friends.

The kids laughed shyly. This was the first soldier I had met.

"*Oslo . . . wunderschön.*" Oslo is very beautiful.

The kids seemed not to understand. I translated into Norwegian for them.

I asked him where he was from.

"*München*."

"*Gut*," I said, impressing him with my German. He didn't look much older than Jon or I. He was here in charge of our park now. Keeping us out and his tanks in. I had the schoolbook German to say something. I just couldn't think of what to say. Should I ask him if this was his first invasion? How many women he had raped? Why I couldn't go where I chose in my own city?

One of the little kids, a wiry boy of eleven or twelve, scooted under the rope and ran toward the tanks while we were talking. "*Halt! Halt!*" the soldier yelled, but the kid kept running. He touched the nearest tank as you would touch base in a game of tag. He looked back at his friend, triumphant, and then he skipped off across the park.

"*Dummer Norweger!*" the guard said to no one in particular. He raised his rifle and fired a shot into the air. At that the kid began to duck and dodge and run close to the ground. He was only halfway across the play yard. There were guards coming toward him from the other side. Out from the tanks soldiers ran, some with rifles. The boy was obviously penned in.

"Halt!" said the young soldier we had been talking to. After firing that shot he seemed different to me. He must have sounded different to the boy, too.

There was no way to escape. The little wiseguy stopped and sort of shrugged in the middle of the playground. The first soldier to him hit the boy in the gut with his rifle butt. The boy came feet off the ground and then dropped flat and shocked on his ass. Two soldiers grabbed him by the arms and hoisted him twisting and kicking in among the tanks.

"Raus, verdammt . . . los, los!" the young guard snarled at us, telling us to clear out.

"You're a great watchdog. Don't let anybody hurt those poor little tanks," Jon yelled in Norwegian when we were safely across the street.

The park where we'd played since we were six was theirs. I

wondered whether the kid had taken a dare, was trying to impress someone, or was trying to get back at the Nazis somehow. We were glum and sober, thinking what it would cost him.

It was early May; the schools were closed. Jon and I were free, but that's not how we felt.

"Now that you don't need me to do your math homework anymore, can we still be friends?" Jon asked. We couldn't roam the city, play in the park, take trips to the country, explore the skerries. What use was it to be out of school? I told Jon about the planes I'd seen shuttling troops and tanks and guns into Fornebu Airport.

"And I know some of them crashed."

We decided to go to the airport, and our only close call on the trip came when we were cutting through a series of back-yards to get around one of the two major checkpoints. Just as we were about to boost our bikes over the fence between two yards, a man came out and yelled at us. We told him the Nazis were after us. (We didn't know about Norwegian Nazis then.)

"I don't give a damn who's after you. Stay the hell out of my yard."

Jon led the way, quietly retreating. In the old days we would have gotten in a shouting match, gotten our revenge some-how. But things had changed. We looked only for the safest way around.

Getting inside the airport compound was impossible, but the crashes had been in the woods around it. We hid our bikes about a mile from the airport gate and cut off diagonally into the trees. The forest wasn't very thick. We moved easily enough toward the approach path.

We searched for fifteen minutes or so. Jon began to look as though he didn't believe me, and then he spotted a tail stand-ing up in some trees. It belonged to one of the Junkers Tri-motor transports that were the shuttle buses of the invasion. Its wings were twisted and sheared by the trees, but its nose and cockpit were hardly damaged. I thought its broken fuselage panels looked more like pieces of corrugated roof than part of a mighty war machine. Inside I thought I saw blood, on the pilot's seat, but there wasn't very much of it. Everything was stripped from the wreck. There were no guns in the turrets, not even seat belts in the cockpit. Faint but noticeable, a sharp, sick smell like smoke from an electrical fire hung over the wreck.

We went deeper into the woods. Ahead was a charred sort of clearing burned crispy black, oily black. The souvenirs are burned, I thought. But we rummaged around anyway. It was a grim scene, but exciting. Like the tanks, these transports were a novelty, the first warplanes we'd seen up close. We were boys on a holiday, but it was more than boyish curiosity now when we looked at war machines.

The third crash was an M-109. The fighter had buried itself right back to the wings. The crumpled metal where the plane met the ground was a compressed amalgam of engine, cockpit, and . . . pilot? I suppose we could have pulled the metal aside for a better look, but we didn't. I saw a propeller blade tip sticking out from the mangled mass. I tugged on it and it came away. Sticking to it was a glob. I first thought it was tar. It was a hand . . . a severed hand. The wristbone was yellow, like an old dog bone. It looked like a seared lamb chop. It was so strange-looking that I didn't feel much—not horror, not sympathy. Neither of us knew what to do with it, so I put it back.

We had to hunt for the last wreck, but it was the best. We found cannon-shell casing, silver buttons, the flap from a leather flight helmet, and a broken field radio. Then we left for home.

We really didn't have to go that far to fulfill our military curiosity. Ugly as they were, the hateful weapons of a hateful enemy were all around. Especially the tanks. The roar of their huge engines was beautiful. It reminded me of storm surf, far off, constant, deep, destructive, alluring. Wretched black monster beetles. How the hell could we fight them?

Files of soldiers, fifty, a hundred, sometimes more, marched everywhere. From the invasion right through the summer they marched in the Oslo streets. They were not marching to duty stations. Their duty was to march, and sing. "*Dann wir fahren gegen Engeland*"—and next we go to England. Mausers with fixed bayonets, full regalia, silver buckles inscribed "*Gott mitt uns*"—God is with us. They made it seem as if Nazi soldiers were in endless supply.

The king's Royal Guard were the focus of much of our national pride. We once celebrated them for their precision, their expertise, and their bearing, and for bringing the Viking legends forward into the twentieth century. They were the cream of Norway's soldiers. My mother and I were walking one day along one of the edges of the Royal Palace grounds. We both noticed a file of Norwegian prisoners being marched along. We saw they were Royal Guards. Watching these proud men, the best of our fighters, herded around the palace they used to guard made us very sad. I felt my mother's hand on my shoulder. I turned and saw her weeping openly. Painful sights and humiliations came for all of us with the occupation.

One of the first signs of resistance was sign-painting: a V for victory enclosing H and the number 7 (for King Haakon VII). Less than four months after the invasion, the Nazi-installed Norwegian administrative council called for the king to abdicate. A low and confusing time it was, when his own countrymen, even puppet countrymen, asked their king to resign. King Haakon might have been forced into stating that his countrymen didn't want a government in exile, didn't want him.

I began to see that each of those signs was much more than graffiti, or even a message of opposition to the Nazis, of wishful thinking. We were "voting" for the king with those signs, letting the world know, letting the king know, that we were loyal still and that that the quislings were speaking only for themselves. The people in Norway had not abandoned their king, and they were hoping he wouldn't be forced into abdicating. I feel sure our "votes" cast on walls and pillars and signposts helped King Haakon maintain his right. I can still remember listening to his sober, eloquent letter of reply to the council's demand for his abdication. He read it himself over the BBC transmission to Norway: "My duty is to uphold the nation's sovereignty until free and normal constitutional processes can be resumed." We wept and cheered when we heard it.

It took a long while for us to recover from the shock of the invasion. It took a very long while to figure out how to fight back. Nonetheless, during all of that time solidarity was building.

Norwegians refused to sit with soldiers on the trams. Wearing a paper clip in your lapel became a signal of loyalty to the king. At the end of 1940, after our "liberators" had done their best to woo us, their "Nordic cousins," into collaboration, there were still only *twenty thousand* Norwegians (out of our population of three and a half million) actively collaborating with the Nazis.

The Reich wanted tight control and "no trouble in Norway." Hitler wanted our resources, our help in the war effort, our strategic naval advantages. And he wanted to steal away an ally from England. But he couldn't afford to tie up a large occupying army; nor could he afford to let us live so free that we might entertain an uprising. All of this led to the second phase of the German invasion, which the invaders called Nazification.

One of the first new orders was formation of a Norwegian Sports Association. It was controlled by the Nazis. To take part in any public sport you had to join. The reaction was a spontaneous "sports strike." It lasted through the war. No one took part in sports. With only collaborators to draw from, most sports dried up. The ones that continued, ski racing for one, became a joke.

Terboven was the Nazi Gauleiter, Quisling was the Nor-

wegian figurehead, but the main figure in Nazification was
Hagelin, Quisling's second-in-command. Hagelin had spent
many years in Germany as a businessman. He came back
"home" full of admiration for what Hitler had done, deter-
mined to carry out the same "social and economic miracles"
in Norway. The king and the parliament had been chased into
exile, but we still had a strong system of mayors and local
officials. Hagelin's "Führer principle" meant replacing elected
officials with ones he would appoint in the Führer's name. In
many cases, though, he could find no one to appoint. In others, he chose to reappoint existing mayors. My father knew
several men, one from our island, who were caught in this
"Hagelin's choice." They could show their loyalty to Norway
and the king by refusing to serve, and letting local government
fall away or into the hands of Quisling goons. Or they could
serve under the new system—collaborate, in fact—which would
allow government to continue and probably place them in a
better spot to "resist from within." Some men chose stiff,
uncompromising resistance. Others tried to be more flexible.
The big pressure on us was not to split apart over these differences. As the occupation went on the Nazis' policies made
solidarity easier.

A spontaneous workers' strike in Oslo over withholding milk
rations for factory workers finally caused the Gestapo to take
its gloves off. The strikers had actually voted to go back to work
when the police struck. Streets were barricaded, factories ransacked, workers arrested, leaders jailed; the storm troopers came
out in numbers never before seen in Norway. Two young trade-
union officials, both of whom had attempted to persuade the
workers to return to their jobs, were arrested and sentenced by
the police tribunal to death. It was a typical occasion of Nazi
"justice": while the tribunal deliberated the two were already
dead, executed the previous evening by a Gestapo firing squad.

Quisling forced the justices of Norway's supreme court to
resign, but not before the well-respected judges denounced the

"new order" as "basically lawless." The Nazis tried to enroll
the church, particularly the Lutheran State Church, to which
an overwhelming number of Norwegians belonged, on their
side, but church leaders formed a common front, preached
against the violence of the Quisling youth squads (hirds), and
gave Quisling little choice but to create his own Nazified
"Church of Norway." The Nazi churches remained empty while
"illegal" pastors preached to full churches. People came both
for spiritual solace in troubled times and to protest against the
invaders.

In 1942, Quisling set up the Riksting, a governing body
with members appointed from civil and labor groups. Loyal
Norwegians then withdrew from those groups, leaving Quisling still no closer to Nazifying our society.

Our school was shut down in February of 1942. They told
us that it was to save fuel, that school would open when the
weather got warmer. Actually the teachers, twelve thousand of
the fourteen thousand in the country, went on strike when
Quisling formed the National Socialist Youth Federation and
tried to force them to "promote students' understanding of the
new ideology and view of society of the Norwegian Nazi Party."
Almost fifteen hundred teachers were arrested. One group of
five hundred was sent to a labor camp north of the Arctic Circle, where many died and all suffered greatly. Despite (or maybe
because of) the Gestapo's heavy hand, the strike held out until
the youth-federation proposal was abandoned.

Food in Oslo was plentiful enough at the beginning of the
occupation. Then we had two tough winters and our overlords
invaded Russia. Beef had long ago disappeared, and so had
fresh fruit. We got occasional fish, and potatoes and onions
were still available, but things were very tight. Sugar was like
gold. So was coffee. We could produce some things—chickens, turnips, cabbage, etc.—and fool the ration police, but
everything that was officially rationed was in agonizingly short
supply. Still, almost everyone had an uncounted chicken, an

extra piglet, a gallon of milk, "for the king." The SS tallied and took what food it found.

Still, when I went through my growing spurt from five feet six to six feet two, I didn't have nearly as much to eat as my wobbly legs, light head, and growling stomach would have liked. If I saw another turnip fried in margarine ("It tastes just like steak"), I thought, I'd start sprouting greens out my ears.

The school strike came as a blessing. Not only did I not have to worry about math homework for a while, but my family, with five to feed on dwindling rations, sent me to live for the duration on my uncle's farm in the center of the country.

It was just what I'd hoped it would be. I tended cows, milked them, and had almost as much milk to drink as I wanted. We had whole-grain flour for delicious bread. I worked in the garden for the carrots I raised. It was as if the war never happened.

The country around the farm was glorious, we had lots of work to keep us busy, and life seemed very much like the old days. There were lakes all around. We would ride out to fish almost every day, swim, or just explore. My growth spurt left me weak. My six months in the country fixed that. By the time I got back to Oslo I was in the best shape of my life, which was very good luck indeed.

The Wehrmacht now occupied my old school. My new one, Voss Skole, was an hour's walk across town. We had classes in the morning, afternoon, or evening depending on how we rotated with other schools. I used to walk most of the time with Per. Next to Jon, perhaps, he was my closest friend growing up. He was tall, good-looking, blond, and about six months older. We'd meet at Professor Dahl's gate, near the bottom of my street. Past the biggest girls' school in Oslo and Bislet Stadium, a place where international records in speed skating and track and field fell like flies, That was it for the interesting landmarks, but I used to enjoy our talks. Sometimes we talked about sled dogs. Per's dog was General Wavell, mine was Mette. Both were reisenschnauzers, but they had very different tem-

peraments. Wavell was quiet but fierce. Mette sounded fierce
but was timid.

In school we plotted against Snusen. Snusen was not only
our English teacher, not only a very poor disciplinarian, and
not only extremely boring, he was also a Nazi. But we didn't
do anything much to him until after what happened to Mrs.
Lunden. She was our history teacher, a vibrant, intelligent,
attractive woman. We all loved her. I can still remember
the day in class when she spoke to us for nearly half an hour
about freedom. She discussed some famous struggles for
freedom, to put our own into perspective. The next day she
was gone.

No one from the school would explain what had happened
to her, but we knew she'd been betrayed to the Nazis. We
assumed that it was Snusen. He was just petty enough to turn
in our favorite teacher out of jealousy.

Snusen suffered. Per and I nailed his overshoes to the floor
during one recess. Every time he turned to the board someone
would bounce a five-øre coin off the slate near his ear. The
coins, of course, were symbolic. Each had on it the H7 legend
of our exiled king.

Jon and I put an alarm clock in the ventilation shaft. It went
off like a big explosion in a small mine. Between classes, once,
we screwed a bell underneath my seat and led a string back to
his. When I raised my hand he'd pull the string. We both got
caught and punished for that one.

Our most elaborate revenge was our staging of *Per Gynt*,
the Norwegian national myth poem, at Snusen's expense. The
curtain went up (at a signal from our classmate Per) and the
whole class, heads down, lips tight, books open in front of us,
hummed for Snusen—"Ba bum, ba bum, ba ba ba ba ba
bum"—from Grieg's music. Then, when Snusen had his red
beard twitching and his red face screwed out of shape trying to
stop the symphony, we released the air-raid curtains and plunged
the room into darkness, which brought the finale, a rain of

five-øre pieces and the metamorphosis of a symphonic score into a barnyard rut.

Our nastiest prank was setting the wood fence around the school on fire. That one we got away with.

There was a quiet, bookish student in our class. He was named Knut, I think, Knut Granlund. Not too long after Mrs. Lunden was taken away, Knut stopped coming to class. It became obvious that he must have been a Nazi informer. It must have been thanks to him with that Mrs. Lunden was arrested. The only good thing about Knut is that he made Snusen look good, and we were easier on him from then on.

Toward the end of 1943 the Swedish Red Cross succeeded, after years of trying, in getting the Nazis to accept humanitarian parcels for the children of Norway. The deliveries included concentrated-soup ingredients and a sort of imitation honey. We had a shipment in the basement of Voss Skole. Just before Christmas, full of the spirit, we broke into the cellar and stole two containers of honey.

It was a treat on bread, on turnips, off the back of your hand, but we had a plan. We got hold of some yeast, and in the chemistry lab that I had at home we organized a little still. With mishaps of one kind or another it took a couple of weeks, but finally we had a brew. It had quite a bite. It smelled like rotten fruit and tasted like metal polish, but it did have quite a bite. We cut it in jugs with ersatz orange juice (which wasn't so wonderful itself), and there was our holiday cheer.

One evening in my flat several of us were sampling the concoction. Somehow the plan for a party bubbled forth. Jan Naerup said that his house was available, Jon's brother was a baker and he thought we could wangle something to eat, Per thought he could get hold of some herring before then. Erik, Lippe, and I had "forbidden" records—Glenn Miller, Tommy Dorsey, and Benny Goodman. We had our miraculous hooch.

"Why don't we have a dancing party?"

"Where the hell will we get the girls?" Per asked, voicing

he lurking doubt that all of us felt. Nobody knew. We took
some more pulls of orange-blossom death, and the party idea
seemed to fade into the background. It was such a good idea,
hough, that each of us tried to revive it somehow. I think it
was Per who pointed out the strength in our numbers and
pushed us to take the action we did. At any rate, we struck out,
en masse, to solve the problem of no girls. All of us went
together to the girls' school near my house. We walked up to
he prettiest ones, told them about our party, and asked them
f they would like to come. Not only would they like to—they
did.

The only problem was Per. He met a lovely black-haired
girl. He hit it off very well with her, but then he asked her
where she lived. She told him. It was at least an hour's walk
from Jan's. That's when he told her about his asthma, his hives,
and his running sores. In three more minutes he found a short,
perky blonde who lived much closer. Her name was Reidun.

There probably weren't many other parties in Oslo that Sat-
urday night. We picked up the girls and arrived at Jan's. The
blackout curtains were already down. Most boy-girl parties have
their awkward stages, especially when everyone is on some sort
of blind date, but when our girls arrived and saw the food, the
herring cake Per's mother had made, and especially the white-
flour cake iced with surrogate cream that Jon's brother had
made, there was no awkwardness at all. They just began eating. We simply joined in.

Jon's brother made a small sugar figure of a reisenschnauzer
to decorate the cake. Some of the girls had heard about sled
dog teams, seen them in the mountains, but we gave them the
real story. We called our little group the Northwind Gusts. In
the blustering spirit of Arctic sledgedom we sang songs. Almost
all of them were about ourselves, of course. We toasted our
dogs and roasted one another and captivated (we were certain)
each fluttering feminine heart with our boldness, cleverness,
and style.

I think we were through, but at any rate we were all surprised when Reidun, with her high cheekbones and single golden braid, got up. "This talk of mighty men, these tales of hearty dogs! I am inspired. Hear ye now the saga of Reidun and Tilse."

And she proceeded to treat us to the hilarious and somehow suggestive tale of a girl and her cat. If there was any ice to be broken, it had vanished by the time we rose to give Reidun and her noble feline, whiskers ice-crushed, paws sore from stalking across the frozen tundra, a rousing ovation. When Per then rose to speak about the sad story of his pet turtle and its ultimate end in a glorious soup, the crowd reaction was just as raucous but much less positive.

The time between those opening toasts and "Good-night Ladies" was glorious. The Norse tradition of a welcoming speech to the ladies is taken seriously, even at parties like ours. No one had the guts to address the women alone, so we made up a song and sang it together.

Sidsel, a buxom, blue-eyed charmer who smoked an elegant pipe (stuffed with the standard wartime blend of tobacco extended with chicory and corn husks), seemed the self appointed speaker in response to our "song." We had intended some kind of polite courtesy to get the thing over with. Sidsel spoke seriously. It was hard to tell if she were angry, or nervous, or what. "You are such brave men—you drag your women off by the hair, you feed them mildew liquor, you tell them of your mighty dogs. But none is brave enough to speak for himself."

Jon had been sitting with Sidsel and talking to her. He had walked her to the party. I tried to catch his eye to see what this lady was up to. He gave me a shrug. Was she offended? Was she getting ready to leave?

"I am just a poor girl, but for myself I say that you may drag me by the hair so long as you don't pull too hard, you may spend time with your dogs if you bathe afterward, and you may

eed me horse piddle to drink if there is nothing better. But,
ut my valiant Norse warriors, if, as rumor suggests, there is
omething here to drink besides this orange death, I sincerely
1ope that you gentlemen won't make me and my friends drink
his panther pulp any longer."

I didn't know what she meant. I looked at Per. He was blank,
Then, slyly, Jon pulled from under the pile of coats by the
loor a very fancy bottle. In his best *sommelier* imitation:
Madmoiselle, it is my great pleasure to introduce you to Grande
Charme, sparkling wine from the rhubarb. 1939, an excellent
ear. Perhaps one of the three such vintage bottles left in
ccupied Norway."

We were gentlemen enough to let the ladies drink it, but
hey paid. The Northwind Gusts once again banded together
n pulpy solidarity. We gave the ladies our sled driver's litany:

"He has at least one glass of sulfuric acid every morning."

"He wears barbed-wire underwear."

"He fixes his collar with a nail, right"—and we'd simulta-
eously spike the back of our necks—"here."

"He gives his food to his dogs and exists upon rock, stars,
nd clouds . . . he makes do with the basics."

Behind the blackout curtains, tucked away near the end of
dead-end street, we didn't think anyone would discover our
ecret party. Still, if they did, who knew what penalties the
tapo would delight in coming up with? Dancing, "decadent"
azz and swing, were absolutely forbidden by the Nazis. Stapo
ould certainly take our food and our records. They might
ven lock some people up. We'd heard of the kids being arrested
or smiling and holding hands on the tram. We were more
han smiling, and soon we hoped we'd be more than holding
ands.

In any case, we retired the Northwind Gusts for the night
nd brought out Glenn Miller. The smooth sounds called us
ll out onto the improvised dance floor in Jan's dining room.
here was no shyness, no coquetry. We all wanted to dance,

and so we danced. Each of us had walked one of the girls to the party. Already the pairings looked a little off. In fact, I could tell that my two best friends each had an eye on Reidun even though Per had brought her to the party and Jon had escorted Sidsel. They traded off dances, I hugged Jorun. She was nearly as tall as I, but she had round firmness in places where I most certainly didn't.

I was a little drunk, maybe drunker than anyone, actually, since it was my brew and I had to prove how tasty it was, but it was a pleasant feeling, a warmth. I may have been the drunkest, but I wasn't very drunk at all. I still remember things about that night after almost half a century. Maybe I make it into something more wonderful than it was, maybe I romanticize, maybe there were humdrum moments that I don't recall, but I remember that it was wonderful. Jorun held me tight, the music set a pace we all felt, all swung to, and we seemed like a family, a big tribe, a band of brothers and sisters. Closed behind curtains, hiding from the Stapo, we shut out the ugly realities out there. The tingle of sex and discovery that was in the air didn't fragment us. It was like a brew, much better than mine, that we all drank from.

We were all quite inexperienced sexually. Couples didn't sneak off. It was Oslo winter outside, Jan's parents were upstairs, it was a small house . . . there was nowhere to go. We danced close and romantically, but we all talked, to our partners, to other couples. I felt such affection for everyone. The boys I'd grown up with. These wonderful women, all equally mysterious, grown-up, and adventurous. Was this what it was like when you grew up? I wanted us to stay laughing, hugging, drinking, joking . . . I didn't want the music to stop at all. don't think any of us did.

I tried hard to steal a kiss from Jorun while we danced. Before long it was not a question of stealing. Yes, yes, yes, indeed. opened my eyes at one point, a smile as big as I was wrapped all around me, and I noticed Reidun sitting on Jon's lap. Th perky little lady had come with Per. I knew Per's temper, I knew the pride of both of my best friends, I began to worry. Then I turned on the dance floor, and across the room were Per and Sidsel stretched out together, Per's head pillowed on Sidsel's ample chest. I've heard in excruciating detail how the "switch" came about, but back then all I knew was that instead of the bubble being broken and my best friends cutting each other's hearts out, everyone was happy and our little ship might keep sailing a little longer. And so it did until, when midnight came, we walked our separate ways into the cold and dark.

Chapter Eight

It is morning on the Grand Banks. Chris has the deck watch. Tone just came below looking like a drowned rat. "Bad out there, huh?"

"It's not so bad, Bels. It's raining, but the fog seems to have washed away. Visibility is something like a mile. A nice little breeze, too. Still out of the west. I thought west was the fair-weather breeze."

"It is, but you can get lows embedded in the westerly flow, and they stack up out here in the ocean. Something like that. When I'm finished writing I'll have to see if I can find something about these weather patterns in the Book."

"The Book" to us is Bowditch—*The American Practical Navigator*, by Nathaniel Bowditch. It's all in there. Whatever you want or need to know about ships and the sea, and weather, too, it's in there. I've got a fair grasp of the weather, certainly enough to get by, but reading the Book puts it all in such clear perspective. I feel as if I'm seeing things for the first time.

Tone fumbles in the galley and comes away with a grape-
fruit-sized chunk of bread.

"You can't eat that unless you promise to bake more."

"No rest for the wicked," she says. "Speaking of which, skipper, where's my reward?"

"Oh, for enduring a long morning watch in no sun and
much rain? For keeping us pointed at the lochs? Aha, just a
minute." I pull out our ship's scotch and slosh her two fingers
in a water glass, neat. "Sleep tight, little baker lady—you look
like you've earned this."

She sits in her long johns on the edge of her berth, caught
in that delicious tension between reward and eiderdown. I can
see her struggling to stay awake long enough to enjoy the golden
glow of her scotch. Ah, life is hell on the open sea.

I sit forward, close to the Tiny Tot stove. It's great the way
it dries things out down below. There have been times this trip
when my hands were sponges—I'd wipe them dry and water
would just ooze out of my fingers again. The atmosphere below
is much better now.

The log book isn't great literature. It combines weather
observation and dead-reckoning data with some thoughts "for
the record" about what's been going on on deck. And we keep
a running tally of the distance left to our landfall at the Caledonian Canal. Today, July 27, I make it just over sixteen
hundred miles to go. We make entries every half hour into
the deck log—wind speed, boat speed, course made good, etc.
Then when someone's finished a watch he or she transfers
thoughts and data to the ship's log. Chris is precise and
sailorly:

> July 20
> 0800   Walker log deployed 22 miles 068 degrees true from
>   Boston Light. 18–22 NNW . . . seas 1–2 meters.
>   Main & No. 2, average 7.2 knots over four hours.
> 0900   . . . surfing at times . . . avg. speed 7.5.

1000   . . . too heavy for steering gear . . . wind due north
       . . . lightening to steady 15, avg. speed 7.0.

Tone writes in a bold hand. Her entries are more elaborate:

       July 20
1100   Woke up underway. I was mad at first. I wanted to
       see something of Boston. Beautiful day, though.
       Breakfast of cereal and some fresh strawberries. . . .
       Breeze continues to lighten. 12–15 now since I've
       been on deck. Chris left me a simple watch . . . just
       steer and watch the waves. . . . Just caught last
       glimpse of land—Provincetown. We must be fifteen
       miles off and we can see the pinpoint of the light-
       house there.
1200   . . . Walker log is turning a bit fast according to the
       DR. When Chris gets his noon sight worked out and
       checks it with loran and radio we should know how
       well it's keeping track of the miles.

The Walker log is old-time sailing machinery, basically an
odometer. It counts the miles you sail by keeping track of the
revolutions of the metal spinner we set out astern, swiveling at
the end of its thirty-yard tether. We hoped our fish would follow us all the way across the ocean, but that hit-and-run trawler last night cut it loose. We have an extra. Chris and I rigged
it at first light. Sharks eat them sometimes, which is why ours
are painted black so they won't flash like a real fish.

I have been trying all morning to put the near-ramming
incident down in our log. And I've been thinking what might
have happened if the ignition hadn't caught. It still sets me
trembling. We wouldn't necessarily have been sunk without a
trace. I've heard stories of sailboats being rammed by super-
tankers; you can be picked up and thrown aside by the bow
wave and live to tell the tale. I had a good friend who was

delivering a boat through the East River in New York. His engine quit just as a barge was coming up behind him. The tug pushed the barge right on top of my friend, and he couldn't get out of its way. He jumped down the companion way. His boat was knocked on its side. It refused to roll under and finally shot out sideways like a squeezed orange pit, and my friend, big boatyard and laundry bills aside, was as good as new. You never know.

All three of us ran out of things to say pretty quickly last night, and we talked again at breakfast, but all we have are questions. It's hard to imagine anyone playing that kind of joke. Tone thought they were working fishermen who thought "yachties" on a sailboat were fair game. Chris thought it might have had something to do with drugs or smuggling. Could they have mistaken us for their rendezvous boat?

I suppose they could have been drunk. But that trawler was sure steering straight when she headed for *Tresbelle*; and Tone thought she heard laughter.

July 26

1300   Mysterious bow wave in fog turned out to be feeding pollack. Caught eight and half-bucket octopi.

1400   light sou'east, 4-8, thick fog, lots of traffic . . . still on 068.

1500   close call with Russian trawler on starboard bow . . . 50–60 meters off.

1600   fog lifted some. Vis = half-mile 068 avging 4 knots.

1700   traffic thick . . . fog horn becoming annoying. 075 avg. (sharpened up to keep speed up to 3.5 knot average) . . . sou'easter off to 2–5 knots.

1800   chum slick or something oily on water. Fog back in. Light drizzle. 3 knots made good on 075.

1900   Chris relieved me early so I could make dinner.

2000   Aromas from galley hard to resist. Boat makes between

	2–3 knots. Would set drifter but not with traffic around.
2100	Dinner in cockpit. Four stars . . . make that five!
2200	2 knots hard on breeze. Off to 055.
2300	Breeze freshens and lifts. Back to 068, averaging 3 knots.
2400	Quiet out here at last. Constant sou'east, constant 4 knots.
0100	Tone on watch. Trawler approaches from astern, shadows us, then turns and powers at us. Arne started engine and we power clear. We notice he cut log spinner from pennant. No clues on trawler ID or motive.

I've been writing daily to Ellen. It makes me feel close to her to think and write. I don't know what to say about the trawler.

Should I tell her about it? That's the kind of thing that would make me worry if I were her. Of course, we'll be in Scotland when she reads anything from me. Just the same . . .

But when she reads this, of course, we'll be safe. Holding back, even out of consideration, can kill love. I think of Ellen coming to me fresh from the shower, and there's nothing for me to hold back. She's inside me, and I can't hold that part back. I don't want to have something to keep from Ellen, something to hide, no matter if it's for her own good. Or maybe I just don't want to make it any more real than it is for myself by describing it to her. Imagine, an old guy like me, sitting here with my seaboots off by the stove wondering what to put in a love letter.

What's it matter? A love letter, a log book, a war story?

I know something that never dies. The story about how you die.

"You're not writing much, Bels."

"Go to sleep, Tone. I'm thinking."

"Maybe when something that extraordinary happens I should stay awake and watch." She yawned around her gamin grin. "Let me get Chris some tea. It's a bitch up there. Then will you tell me a bedtime story?"

"I'm just thinking about that trawler."

"I know, Bels. I didn't really understand all of it while it was happening. I just reacted. Wait . . . let me deliver this to the driver. I'll be right back."

When she returned, she went on talking about it. "I was trying to say how it didn't really affect me when it was going on. Not sheer terror or anything. Now I think of it and it makes me shaky, all hollow. But it's curious . . . I shouldn't say so, but it's strange to see you so upset. I mean, you've seen so much and done so much. You've certainly had close calls."

"That's sort of what we were talking about last night after dinner. If you learn to love life more, it threatens you more to lose it . . . or something like that. At any rate, I can tell you that being a survivor doesn't build up any calluses that make it easier the next time. The other way around, if anything."

"To me the real tragedy would be dying at twenty-five before I get to do half of what you have."

"*Tragique, vraiment tragique*, my dear. I suppose you can find some good side to dying, some 'never a sparrow falls,' but to me it's bitter and ugly and awful. I can't accept death snuffing out life . . . anywhere, ever."

"I don't know, Bels. I mean, life and death are all part of the same process. You can't have one without the other, true?"

"It's hard for me to tell. Understanding death or witnessing it or even being slathered all over with it as I was in the camps doesn't change my feeling that life is what's important."

"Well, sure, that's what every animal feels, that's the instinct in everything for self-preservation, but there are some ways of looking at it that help you understand death, aren't there?"

"Sure, there are heavens of all sizes and kinds for me not to believe in, but life I know is a real thing."

"So's death, though."

"I'm not so sure I don't agree with you."

From topside: "Anybody awake enough to come get this mug?"

"The voice of reality himself," Tone says as she pops up the companionway. She quickly returned.

"You know, not to keep talking about the untalkable things, but I was forced into deadness, into a numbness like death, after my year with the Nazis. The camps took everything live away from me except my heartbeat. They took my feelings, my reactions, reflexes, instincts. They called us 'the already dead,' which of course we weren't, but I was certainly more than half dead. When I got home from Germany right after the end of the war there was a big funeral for Jon and Per and Lars. They found their remains, cremated them, and we buried them. They were my best friends. But I felt nothing. All of Oslo wept, but I never cried. I just marched with Jon's urn with his ashes up to the grave, put them in, and walked away. My best friend. That was awful."

"But you weren't yourself. You'd just gotten out of the death camps."

"Who knows what death is like? But I came close to living it, and there's nothing religious or philosophical you can say to make it good. It may be 'nature's way,' but it's also nature's way to fight like hell against it."

"You think when your friends were shot, then, they should have been weeping and screaming instead of calm, as you described them?"

"No, you're right. They were very calm, very . . . complete."

"Didn't you tell me that you admired them for that?"

"Yes."

"I know this is stupid, but what you were saying, just then, about your friends, it reminded me of something from Shakespeare."

"Shakespeare? I know you studied literature, but that was Jon and Lars, and Per."

"Yes, there's a quote about the 'ripeness' or the 'readiness' . . . yes, 'the readiness is all.' "

"That does sound familiar."

"Yes, that's it. 'The readiness is all.' I think it's Hamlet when he finally kills the king, but people use it to sort of sum up everything they think Shakespeare was about. What came to my mind when you said 'complete' and 'ready to die' really was 'the readiness is all.' It helps me understand Jon and Per and Lars—what they were feeling when they were so calm. I mean, we were talking about the life force, the life instinct, fighting for life, but it can't win, it never wins, does it? So how can anyone win? I think there's the way your friends did. Death got them, but it didn't get to them. Does that make any sense, Bels?"

"I think that it does," I said. "The sailors and marines on *Blücher* . . . they were just as young. But they were coming into a virtually undefended country on one of the world's most powerful battle machines. How could they be ready? The men on the *Blücher* suffocated with boiling bunker oil, sucked to the depths of Drøbak Sound . . . how could they have been ready? Two rounds from ancient guns set in place before World War I and two thousand or more men die.

"It's a wonderful David and Goliath story, and I'm proud we were successful defending ourselves. There's some poetic justice to ambushing the Kriegsmarine in the middle of its sneak attack on us—the rapers getting raped. But the quickness, the irony of it . . . how could they possibly have been 'ready' for that?"

"There may be stranger things in heaven and earth. Armed with all this philosophy, why aren't you writing your war story?" Tone said.

"I don't know. When those sailors, those teenagers, were being burned and killed, I was shivering in my bed. I was sick with fright. I certainly wasn't 'ready.' Maybe when that trawler came at us I was a bit readier. Who the hell knows? Why write? Write what? Who would read it? Would you read it?"

"Christ, I'd write it for you if I could!"

"Are you serious?"

"Of course."

"Maybe I should start by writing to Ellen about the trawler."

"I'll help you with the war story, but you've got to do your own damn love letters, skipper."

Chapter Nine

Our sled dog club was a casualty of the invasion. "Business as usual" just wasn't right under the Nazis. Along with the cinema strike and the sports boycott, we discontinued the sled dog club. However, by the third winter of Nazi occupation, 1942–43, it was revived. There was a need for it. The hills around Oslo fill up with snow in the winter. Many places are reachable only by dogsled. Emergency food after blizzards, mail in and out . . . we were needed. Our main purpose was the same as in the old days, ambulance work. Even though we had a sports strike and there was no ski jumping or racing, people still skiied, and when people ski, some of them break their legs.

The Nazis took no responsibility in such emergencies, so we persuaded the Norwegian Nazi administration that we could solve the problem. It was nice to be able to have dogs. And we got a double ration of dried fish to feed them. (More than once the drivers feasted on "dogfood chowder.") And, just think, instead of being penned in our neighborhoods we had the run of the hills. We got days off from school, spent weekends up there, and generally lived a freer life than we had for a long time.

The sleds were very professional beds or platforms with long skis as runners and tied together with rawhide laces. They had bamboo pulling poles, and we'd use a string of three or four dogs, in single file, to pull them. We wore short skis—good for pushing and climbing and not bad on the downhill, but slow on the flats compared to our normal touring skis. But then we had very few flats in the hills around Oslo.

Jon, Per, Jan, Erik, Lippe, and I all helped get the club going again. We all felt the suspicion of the Stapo. Even though we had official permission, sometimes the Stapo questioned our papers. It turned out that they had good reason to be suspicious. After I was arrested and sent to the camps, there was a period when the British dropped supplies, weapons, radios, and the like to the Mil-Org. The sled dog club then became very important in receiving these drops and transporting them to hiding places. We saw some of the potential of being able to move so freely through the hills. We hoped we'd be called upon to help with escapes or something equally romantic, but while I was there we were almost exclusively ski patrol.

We would take our dogs home with us, of course. They were Alsatians and reisenschnauzers and a team of the famous Greenland dogs. These were descended from the dogs that took Roald Amundsen to the South Pole in 1911. They looked something like huskies, but they were taller and heavier, and they had wonderful long tails that curled up in big letter Cs behind them. They couldn't bark—only cry or howl. Like sled dogs everywhere, they fought among themselves, but not very seriously. When they were pitted against an outside enemy, though, they were very formidable. We called them the Red Team because their coats were a russet color.

I remember one club gathering. It was at night, on a snow-covered lake. Kirsten was with me. While Mette pulled her on her skis, my friend Knut was kind enough to let me drive his Greenland team. Surging and sliding over the snow in the moonlight, calling out the Viking names—"Up, Raude! Come, Ross! Aiii, Raus! Pull, Rørek!"—it was a sled driver's dream.

Even with double rations, we had problems keeping our dogs fed. When they were hungry, they were surly. No one was bitten badly and no children were devoured, but that doesn't mean that it wasn't close. Per's dog was named General Wavell after the leader of the British desert forces in Africa. Christophersen, one of our other friends, named his dog Ruge in honor of the general of the Norwegian army, now a PW. We often wondered what bystanders, maybe even the Stapo thought when they heard "Here, Wavell" or "Ruge, heel." It left very little doubt about our loyalties.

We used to sleep out in the snow quite often. One night I got up to put more wood on the fire. I was bending down to get a log when I heard something. It was sort of like a catch of breath or a short gasp, right behind me. I turned and was instantly belted to the snow beneath seventy-five pounds of reisenschnauzer bitch. Rantas, Jon's unpredictable dog, had her teeth in my sweater at my shoulder. If I hadn't turned, that bite might have come down on the back of my neck.

Wolves will wear their quarry down before they jump for the kill. Rantas was not that sophisticated. She had gnawed through her tether to get loose. She acted, most of the time, as though live worms were gnawing at her brain. For Jon she was smart, strong, and obedient. With the rest of us, and the rest of the world, she was a terror. When I was in the concentration camps, the snarling Alsatians never bothered me. Next to Rantas they seemed like puppies.

The sled dog club was good—the freedom, the adventure, the exploring, the friendship. And it toughened us up. Working with the club wasn't exactly striking a death blow at the Nazi occupation, but it was doing something. And it eventually brought us to the attention of the Oslo Resistance group.

Classes at the Voss Skole were in the afternoon that winter
One day just before Christmas, my friend Jan Naerup cam
quite late. He was scolded and told to stay after school. I wante
to talk to him and see what he'd been up to. My theory wa
that he was spending more time at the girls' schools than a
ours. I never seemed to see him anymore.

During our break we walked to a corner of the schoolyar
to talk. There were little kids milling all around, and a fe
older ones sitting not far away on the wall. We'd been i
schoolyards like this ever since we were the littlest kids. I wa
about to ask him about his girlfriend, but he spoke first.

"Arne," he said, and I became curious because he sounde
so formal, "Arne, I have been asked to ask you if you woul
like to help your country."

I wasn't at all sure what he meant, but I nodded and said
"Of course."

"I am talking, I hope you realize, about the Resistance.
have been asked to ask you if you would like to join. I an
going also to ask Per and Jon. Don't answer now. This is dan
gerous, serious stuff. But don't discuss your decision with any
one, including your family. Let me know by the first of th
year."

We played war with pinecones, we spied on tanks and planes
we wrote the king's victory sign on walls, we were on the edg
of things with the sled dog club. Here was a chance to reall
get in the war. I was flattered. They wanted me! I knew almos
at once that I would do it, but I thought it would seem childis
to say so without taking some time to think it over. The fac
that Jan was willing to wait for my decision made me fee
important, that my choice mattered. How many choices ha
any of us been given since the invasion? Before you worr
about freedom of choice you have to have the freedom to choos
at all. We needed choice back. That's what freedom means
That's what we were fighting for.

I don't think there's any question that I'd do it again. It wa truly not just the right choice, it was the only choice. Each time the Nazis pushed us around they pushed me closer to resisting. I didn't know what it would cost me, but I was quite sure, we all were quite sure, that if we ever were going to be free, we'd have to fight to take our freedom back.

The night after the Stapo arrested me in my bed and took me off to beatings and a solitary cell, I lay there in Akershus trying to sleep. I was exhausted, but I could only sleep in fits and spurts. I ached and throbbed all over. I was scared and anxious, I was worried about the raid and about my friends. In the middle of all of that there was a sort of delirious dream fragment clicking back and forth like a stuck phonograph needle.

The questioner reminded me of Jonas Lie, of my father, of the Stapo inquisitor. His cigar was a rope . . . two-handed, he'd chop, and each time he'd say, "Just say no."

"I won't, I will, I won't say no."

All that night this dialogue kept cropping up. The question asked by these stern poppas was, of course, "Will you ever do it again?"

In my dream, at least, I had courage and control enough to say yes. We were proud to be asked. There was really no choice. Of course we all joined.

Our first day back in school after the New Year I told Jan that I wanted to join. He smiled, but his seriousness was still there. He told me what to do, and he also told me a bit about the Resistance. I knew that orders came from London, and that most of the instructors in Norway had been trained in England. What I didn't know was that there were two branches of the Resistance. The military branch, Mil-Org, was supposed to prepare an underground army either to assist when an Allied invasion came or to carry out a full-scale military uprising. The other branch was the action group. Its mission was disrupting the occupation and sapping the potential of the German war effort however possible. I was going into the action group.

The night was wickedly cold. The stars were like chunks of

glass in the blue-black sky. The moon hadn't come up yet. The north wind was dry and biting. I bundled my way along to the Urianienborg church. To be there before ten o'clock I had to lean into the breeze and hurry. I hurried, and I was panting by the time I got there, but I was on time. I was preoccupied with "South State . . . only South State." I wondered if I should have a pack of South States. I didn't smoke, but wouldn't it be strange not to have them? The thought made me feel amateurish and dumb. Of course I should have brought a pack of cigarettes. Where the hell could I get one now?

My breath was coming in short, shallow pants, not so much from walking against the wind as from the test approaching. I wondered what I should have told my parents. There had to be a better cover story than a meeting of the sled dog club. I'd been in the club for more than a year and we'd had only one meeting in all that time. We'll think of something, I thought.

"South State, only South State."

It was a desolate part of town. At about ten o'clock I went behind the church. I saw a man wrapped up against the cold. I stopped. He waited, patted his pockets, then took a few casual steps toward me.

"Excuse me, but do you have a cigarette?"

"South State," I answered. "Only South State."

"Come with me," he said. No friendliness, no recognition, just "Come with me."

It's a good thing there wasn't anyone else around, because I had no cigarette to give him to make our meeting look as casual as we'd hoped it would. We walked together in silence for about ten minutes. He took me toward the center of Oslo, toward the park. His flat, it turned out, was directly behind the Royal Palace. Quisling now lived there some of the time. When we got there my mouth was dry and my breath was once again coming in sharp, shallow pants. Climbing the stairs to the flat, still in silence, I felt nervous but immensely pleased.

My leader let me through the door and led me through the vestibule into the dining room. Around the table were eight men. I wasn't surprised to see Jon and Per. One other man seemed familiar. The others I didn't recognize. They seemed only a year or two older than my friends and I, but they looked much more at ease. They must be instructors, or old hands at least.

My guide was also our host, and, I found out quickly, the leader of our group. Who was he, I was wondering.

"Welcome, gentlemen. We are beginning a training group tonight. This is what you new men must know. We all have Resistance names." His face was flushed and his eyes sparkled as he spoke. I listened very carefully. "Use only these names. Never refer to or even think of anyone who is with us by any other name. I am Stein Ekberg . . . this is Conrad Hansen . . ." He went around the circle. "And this," he said, motioning to me, "is Karl Gulbrandsen."

It was hard thinking of Jon and Per as Bjarne and Stig, but I tried. Perhaps we were already a security risk because we knew one another's real identities. I worried a little, but the instructors were sharp, fascinating men, and there was so much to learn that I didn't think about it very much. When we were on our own we joked about our new names. Per made fun of my name, pronouncing it like "coral" as in "Karrrlll the undersea sailor," but he never did this where we might be overheard.

Stein lifted out two shelves of lacquerware from the china cabinet. China cabinet? He opened the back with a key. Inside that opening was a sort of chest. A Chinese puzzle. From inside came a Colt .45 for each of the three newcomers and one each for two of the instructors. They broke down their weapons faster than I could believe. Then they assembled them. It seemed to take place inside fifteen seconds. Next it was our turn. We had begun to get the hang of it within about twenty minutes. Then we did it blindfolded. I couldn't help thinking, Yes, I can break it down and put it together, I can break it down and put it together blindfolded, but can I shoot it? Can I hit anything with it?

My initial feeling for the Colt .45 cannon was awe: blue-black death, chunky dynamite, a "horse-stopper." After I'd taken mine apart, fingered the spring, seen inside the chamber, my familiarity bred the opposite of contempt. Because we couldn't practice fire, pulling the trigger on a live round seemed to loom over us like a great mystical rite.

The two instructors who worked with us on the .45 stepped to the background. The other two now explained limpet mines. Stein produced one. We were going over its magnets and how they worked underwater when there was a knock at the door. Limpet mine in hand, Sten guns and .45s on the table—it would be hard to pretend this was a card party. Stein picked up a .45. He rammed home a magazine—*click clack*—and went to the door. Each of the rest of us picked up a gun. If this was the Gestapo, we'd have to shoot our way out.

I looked across at Jon. He was scouting out the garden. The instructors, two to a side, set up high and low inside the vestibule door. I felt the light, businesslike Sten gun in my hand and remembered the instructions. Fire in short bursts. Cover your target with short, side-to-side stitching. Don't spray wildly.

"It's really nice of them to arrange a final exam . . ."

Stein backed away from the door. A middle-aged man entered, alone, unarmed. Stein smiled.

"My father," he said, introducing the man. "He must have forgotten his keys."

The meetings at Stein's continued. The instructors weren't always the same. We knew some had escaped from Norway, been trained in England, and then parachuted back in to train us. We felt a part of something much bigger than ourselves. Some we never saw again. Nothing ever came from our group, but there were rumors that two instructors were killed. When we went over hand grenades, explosives, mines, and things that were really foreign to us, it was much different from being confused in school. From that first night when the knock came

on the apartment door, it was obvious we had to master these
things. Just how soon was a big question.

"Make your hand your weapon," they told us.

We practiced the karate chop and toughened our hands on
walls and boards.

"Use the aggressor's aggression against him," they said.

In the blacked-out basement downtown, mats were broken
out and we had jujitsu lessons. Jon was big and a superb ath-
lete. He was never afraid to mix it up. He was a good boxer
and loved to wrestle. When we were growing up I was almost
a head shorter. They used to tease me a lot. One day when
they got my goat I flew at the kids teasing me, four or five of
them. I didn't give a damn what happened to me; I just wanted
to punish them for being such pricks. It would not have been
very punishing at all if Jon hadn't taken my side. Together we
laid waste to the gang of them. And then I grew. We were now
almost the same size.

Face-to-face jujitsu: I was aggressor. He was supposed to use
my momentum and throw me. He did as he was told, but he
hadn't really figured jujitsu out. He flailingly rolled me over
his hip, but I kept my balance. He grappled me to him, and I
had him by the neck when the instructor stopped us.

The man looked old to me. He must have been around
forty. He looked something like an owl. He had a dome of
snowy white, a beak nose, and glasses. He hawked fiercely at
Jon, "Very sloppy . . . half hearted. Pay attention. Okay,
switch."

Jon was mad now. He came at me hard. I did the hip roll
the way I'd just seen the instructor do it. *Thwack* . . . my best
friend was bounced onto his back. I was afraid I'd knocked him
out. He got up, though, and we switched roles.

"You know the sound of one hand clapping. You know the
speed of a ship with her anchor down. You! You! You must
be present to learn. Without aggression, judo is dancing.
Without letting go, you can never get control. You, you, skinny

one," he said to me. "You have made your friend suffer because you do not match his intensity. A dance with a jellyfish. You, skinny one, don't hurt your friend again."

I was the aggressor now, but so was Jon. He reached for my thrust so hard and early that instead of using my momentum, he stopped it. We were face to face in the middle of the mat. I don't know if we would have punched each other, but the instructor, the eldest of us all at forty or thereabouts, stepped onto our mat.

"With jujitsu there are things to learn and there are things to unlearn. But first, we are building a team here. Don't you two fight each other!"

I'm sure it wasn't apparent to him that we were best friends.

"Don't fight each other. Fight together. Against me." Calmly the graying man faced us both.

"When you're ready," he said. Jon was still steaming, and before I was quite sure what to do he made a vicious thrust. I saw my opportunity and followed it.

Thwack . . . thwack. The sound of two young freedom fighters caressing the mat with their backs.

"You are younger than I, stronger, heavier, but you are on your backs. Pay attention. Be balanced but not flat-footed, alert but not nervous. You have seen your throw before and you must see it when it comes again." The man was not an oriental master, he was Norwegian. He was, in fact, Sigurd Herbern, the man who designed *Tresbelle*.

"Karl, thrust-parry thrust."

Jon's eyes almost glittered at me, they were so icy. I aimed my thrust, as we had been taught, at his solar plexus. In a gathered, catlike roll he dropped his hip and slid aside, grabbed my arm right at the wrist, and rolled up and under my waist . . . lift . . . flip . . . *Thwack.*

"You son of a bitch," I hissed.

"Excellent progress, excellent control," said the instructor. "You gain control of him when you have control of yourself."

We had been training for almost two months when we got our first assignment. It came at the end of a regular session at Stein's flat. He gave us each propaganda leaflets. Bunches of fifty, six bunches to each of us. They were in German, designed to attack the Nazi morale. We were each given target schools, occupied now by German troops, as distribution points.

"These will be much more effective if you get them inside the barracks or the schools themselves," Stein said. "And it must be a synchronized operation. Do it tomorrow night."

My target was the Lakkegata Skole, about ninety minutes' walk from my house. I told my mother that I was going to get some help on my homework. "It's a big test, and I may have to stay pretty late to get ready. Thanks, Mom."

It was March. The air was crisp, but it wasn't unpleasant. I had my leaflets in a briefcase. I had been to the school before. I thought I had a pretty good idea about gates and guardposts and things. I wasn't too sure about getting inside, but I thought I could figure it out. The moon was up, and there was very little wind. It was the kind of stillness that magnifies the sound of a cough or a footstep. Every now and then a tram would clatter by. There were a few cars, but generally people were indoors. There were no streetlights. The blackout curtains were all drawn.

Warm from my walk, my breath in clouds in front of me, I arrived at the school. It was ten o'clock. I tried to look like an innocent schoolboy headed home from late lessons. I walked as casually as I could past the main entrance. I looked in at the guard posted there by the main gate. He certainly knew how to dress for his job. He had on large felt boots that covered his leather boots and a long, thick, green overcoat, and beneath his steel helmet he wore a woolen cap pulled down over his ears. He didn't look like he could run very far or fast, but with the submachine gun over his shoulder, he probably didn't have to.

I walked by the school on the opposite side of the street. He seemed to pay no attention. I could hear Germans talking and boots clicking over the cobblestones of the inner schoolyard. I kept on walking. Finally I got far enough past the gate to cross the street and come around safely behind the school building. Back there was a little fence enclosing some garbage cans. That area was an island of shadows, and I made straight for it. I hopped the fence and hunkered down in the shadow behind the cans. There was space between them and the fence. My heart was beating so loud in my ears that I thought the sentinel out in front of the building could surely hear it. I was gasping, too, from the short run across the open field to the garbage cans. Control, I thought.

Then I heard footsteps. They were heavy, measured, flat-footed steps down the archway leading out the back of the building. German voices were joking. As they got closer I tried to make myself mouselike and invisible between the cans and the fence. Control.

The soldiers were each carrying a pair of full slop buckets. As they strode up to the nearest cans, one let out a grumbling, rumbly fart. They both laughed. The pails clanked, the lids banged, the two joked, and then they went back inside.

What would I say if they caught me here with a briefcase of anti-Reich leaflets?

The thought made my head spin. I was still hunched in a silent ball after the soldiers had gone. For ten minutes or more I stayed frozen. How could I get in? What would happen if I got caught? Where should I go from here? What shall I do with these leaflets? Then in the middle of these questions to myself I heard the high-pitched whine of approaching aircraft. I could tell the sound of RAF bombers. I was wondering what that meant to my mission. Right then something exploded . . . right inside my head!

It was the air-raid siren. The one for the school was on the wall above me, not twenty feet away. It was some kind of reflex, I guess, but I emptied most of the leaflets into the trash cans.

In no time at all I was over the fence, across the street, and two blocks away.

It was against the law to be on the streets during an air raid. I was ninety minutes from home. The antiaircraft guns opened up, the sirens went on, and there I was. It is one thing to be out on the streets at night in an air raid, I thought. It's another to be out on the streets with a briefcase half full of propaganda printed in England. I saw a phone booth and dumped the remaining leaflets inside.

You didn't have to be a Resistance fighter to sneak through the city at night. I'd done it before, and I arrived home around midnight. I felt terrible. I had been so scared. Despite my training, despite such a simple mission, I had been so scared. I had thrown away my leaflets. Some great Resistance fighter! Some great hero!

Mother was up when I got home. I think I was dirtier and sweatier than she might have expected from studying for a test, but she didn't say anything.

"I'm sorry that I'm so late, Mom. We had just finished and then the air raid came. I'm sorry to make you wait up."

She just looked at me. Then she said, "I know you must do what you have to do."

Chapter Ten

Tresbelle has never gone faster, certainly not that I know of. The west wind is a solid thirty now. I look astern and I see white-and-blue agitation all the way to the horizon. The waves are big. The breeze is lopping the tops off them, covering their slopes with spindrift, flecking the sea with foam. Closer under our stern, the wave faces are alive with skittering wind ripples. It is truly blowing. The wind has been building over the past twenty-four hours, bulldozing these big rollers to spectacular height. There are clouds, some sun, an occasional seabird, a solitary jet trail, but we are all concentrating on the wind and waves . . . powerful wind and huge waves.

We're broad-reaching. *Tresbelle* is on port tack (main boom to starboard) and the waves are coming at us from almost directly astern. Even if we had a steerer that worked, I doubt if it could handle these. I try to figure how high they are. When we are in the trough between them, the wave ahead looks higher than our spreaders. Our spreaders are twenty-eight feet off the water. Thirty-footers? Who knows?

One reason the boat is handling so well and going so fast is the balance between our double-reefed mainsail (shrunk in size by over a third) and the number-three jib, which we have winged out to port on the spinnaker pole. The sail combination gives us all the power we could want, yet it's easy to control and there's not a lot of leftover energy to twist and wrack the boat around.

At this rate—160 miles noon-to-noon yesterday—we'll be halfway across by tomorrow, August 1, and only thirteen-hundred miles left. It's twenty-six hundred miles from Boston to the Caledonian Canal. Thirteen hundred miles in twelve days. That's not bad for a little old cruiser like *Tresbelle*. During the TwoStar race the best day that Gustave and Toffen had was 165 miles. Maybe today we cruisers, we sedate old farty cruisers, will shoot down that record.

We are steering 068 for Aran Island off the Irish coast. I say "steering 068" but I am only trying to average something like that on the compass. Keeping the boat going dead straight in this wind and these waves is almost impossible, and it's stupid. The more you crank the rudder back and forth, the more resistance you create. That slows you down. You learn after a while how far to let the boat swing. Most of the time she will come back toward course. Anticipating the swing and keeping her from getting outside her limits are important.

But you can't be too analytical about surfing. It's fast and it's fun. It's not hard, either. As the waves rise up astern, I can see their tops blow and skitter toward me. Call them whitecaps or even combers, the waves are still small enough and solid enough that catching them with *Tresbelle* is fun, not survival. We roll a lot waiting to catch the waves. I rigged something to hold the boom in place, a rubber "snubber," sort of like a shock absorber. It holds the boom down, but if the boom buries in a wave there's enough stretch in the system, we hope, so that if anything breaks it will be the rubber.

I look over my shoulder for the next wave. If they break as they come or come at a funny angle, you've got to compensate. Most of the time I just wait. I look aft over my left shoulder. I feel that weight of the puff on my face, see the run of the wave, feel the port corner of the stern start to lift, and feel a tug on the wheel as *Tresbelle* starts to round to port into the wind. Enough right rudder to keep her straight, look quickly at the compass, feel the puff push us onto the wave, and relax as the pressure comes off the rudder. The *speed jumps up . . . the boat flattens out . . . spray shoots twenty, twenty-five, thirty feet out to either side*. I don't always do it out loud, but I can never catch a wave like this without a shout or a scream. In a race when you've busted your ass all around the course and you're the first one to catch a wave, there's a warwhoop. Even under my breath there's a little "aha!" of satisfaction. And when the speed climbs to fifteen or sixteen knots and the bow's pointed for Ireland . . . aha indeed!

Ride the wave as long as you can . . . steer straight, then straighten her out as she slows in the trough, look over your shoulder. Sometimes the trip down the wave face upsets the equilibrium of sails and rudder, and you tip, drag the pole or boom in the water, and come up shaken and shaking, like a dog that's just climbed out of the water.

I may have ruined Sigurd's career by changing the *Tresbelle*'s bow, but after riding her down these waves I have nothing but admiration for her design. Surfing can really tell you about a sailboat's hidden qualities. Some flat-bottomed boats will plane like a motorboat down the fronts of the waves, but they're just as likely to be charging off to the side or fishtailing about; there is nothing much under the water to keep them going straight. Their speed can be awesome, but steering them can be wicked. Long narrow boats that are fast on other points of sail can be submarines when they're surfing—they just keep going down one wave and through the back of the next. That presents problems.

Tresbelle is a sled. She lifts early and accelerates nicely as the wave comes under her, she breaks loose and charges straight as she catches the wave. Her shape is a balance of curves. She is not imprisoned in the wave. She is more like an otter. She just playfully uses its power to get where she's going. When she overruns the trough and fetches up against the back of the wave ahead, her full (good-looking) bow lifts her and we have a minimum of unsightly green water coming aboard.

I guess the classic test of a sailboat design is how well a boat can "claw off" a lee shore. When the wind and waves are pushing you toward the rocks, it is certainly nice to have a powerful, weatherly boat that can sail herself free. *Tresbelle* is a witch. The few times I've needed her to sail me out of that kind of box she has come through beautifully. I didn't know all of this when I named her "very beautiful," but the more I see, the more beautiful she becomes.

Chris and Tone are with me in the cockpit. It's exciting sailing. Once you get the rhythm of catching the waves, the steering is easy.

Chris in his black sou'wester, Tone in her yellow one, they could have been taken from a dory fishing the Banks a century ago.

"I've told you both about my dream, my nightmare, my screams. About how my three best friends were executed. I wanted to live, and did. They wanted to live, and didn't. I feel guilty that I lived and happy I lived. Maybe that's where the nightmare comes from."

Something about sliding down these waves makes it easy to talk. Not that I can concentrate too well on the waves and on talking, though.

"Do you want to drive?"

"Okay, but listening and driving takes work, too," Tone said. Tone is a natural water person. Her hair almost matching her yellow weather gear, her glinting blue eyes squinted against the glare, her large, thin-lipped mouth drawn down for a wisecrack, exploding into a smile, she looks as though she were born to drive a fifteen-thousand-pound sailboat down three-story waves.

"What I still don't really understand is *how* I lived."

"What do you mean?" Chris asked.

"Well, we were all sentenced to death. I was waiting for the firing squad myself when they were taken away. I was next. When they came to get me the next morning, I knew that was it.

"They took me to Gestapo headquarters at Viktoria Terrasse. I was in a cell in the basement for most of the morning. I had already 'gotten ready' to die. This time I thought mostly of my family, of things I wish I had said to them."

"Not to be the inquisitive journalist, but a question just occurred to me here on God's great ocean—did you pray?" Chris asked.

"No. I never prayed. . . .

Finally they took me upstairs. The offices had a view over the docks. You could see the harbor. The guards delivered me to a *Hauptsturmführer*—an SS captain—who sat behind a tall wooden desk. I was delighted I'd missed the Gestapo chief, Fehmer. It was said that he never got nasty—his manners were always civilized and he showed every semblance of concern for the prisoner—but he administered terrible beatings with a smile. The captain they brought me to had one blue eye and the other was half blue and half black.

He responded oddly to my name: "Arne Lie . . . Arne Lie! *Aber er lebt doch!*" He is still alive!

I guess it was flattering when they raised a commotion on my account, but I was also alarmed. Most of the guards on the floor scurried over to the captain. Then they scattered, talking German too fast for me to understand. I was left alone still standing in front of the captain's desk while everyone else was busy looking in files, leafing through batches of paper, and opening drawers.

The captain returned. *"Du hast Glück gehabt"*—"You have been lucky." This smiling black-and-blue-eyed secret policeman then asked me questions, lots of questions—When was I arrested? Where was my home?—all detached, polite, almost courteous.

I couldn't help but think this must be the famous *Wienerbröd metoden*, "danish pastry," our term for Gestapo sweet talk. I didn't know why they wanted to throw me off balance if they were going to kill me. For the first time since coming to Viktoria Terrasse I allowed myself a bit of hope.

They scurried for a few minutes more, and then the Gestapo activity died away. I was still standing in front of the black-and-blue-eyed man. He repeated that I was lucky. It looked as if nobody could find my papers. A man without papers in the German bureaucracy is a rare and troubling thing, but I couldn't tell what that would mean to me.

It changed my fate so much that in ten minutes the Gestapo was calling home to my family to have them bring me clean clothes.

I still can't understand what really happened. I know my friends and I were arrested separately. I know that they were shot for being in the raid, and I wasn't in the raid—was that why they let me off? Did some Norwegian clerk play with the records in hopes of saving someone? Was it a simple bureaucratic mistake? Was it something to do with the other Resistance prisoners? The Nazis were known to blunt Resistance movements by both executions and "disappearances." Is that why they kept me alive and called my family?

They continued to treat me well. I waited for half an hour, and then my sister came. I wish I really knew why I was let off death row, why my papers were lost. Were the missing papers a miracle? A screw-up? A Gestapo trick? My story still has that big question mark in the middle of it. Even after the war when

we went through the Viktoria Terrasse and Stapo records we
found no new answers.

Chris and I like smoked herring, and are breakfasting or
kippers. Tone is at the helm. The breeze has lightened by half.
"My sister came with my clean clothes. It was like having a
window into life blasted in the walls around me. The door into
life had just opened when it was inches from being closed. I
hadn't talked with anyone I knew or trusted since the Stapo
dragged me out of my bedroom. Then there was Sylvei. It's
hard to describe. But she is more than equal to that. This year
when she heard of my plans for the book, she wrote me a letter
remembering that meeting. Would you read it? I showed it to
Tone last watch.
"Certainly. Sure."

Dear Arne,
    When I think about it, our meeting at Viktoria Terrasse
could not have lasted more than five or six minutes. It
seemed, however, like an eternity, and, speaking for myself,
the overwhelming impressions from that meeting have
molded my attitude to life.
    Your arrest and the events that followed make a simple,
straightforward story. It is the unmentioned, the reactions,
and how one was shaken in one's inner self that are difficult
to describe. Behind the details of, for instance, our meeting
there is a long chain of sad and worrying events that explain
our emotions.
    Occupied by the Germans—our king and a united parlia-
ment had declared war. We had learned the hard way that
"no" was no answer. One did not give up, one had to find
alternatives.
    One ordinary day, Mother called and said, "Arne has been
arrested."

My whole body and soul were in revolt.

I found Mother sitting on a chair in the middle of the kitchen floor, her arms around her knees. She looked like a little island. In her sorrow so alone, nevertheless, so strong. She looked so terribly small. Her face was white and pale. No tears, no hysteria. She told me with a dry, unfamiliar voice what had happened. I understood as follows:

In the middle of the night the door of the apartment burst open. Heavily armed Germans barged into Mother and Father's bedroom and arrested Father. You came out of your bedroom, hands over your head and guns pointing at you, and Father was released. It was obvious that any escape was impossible with so many Germans in the apartment. They were very nervous, but any shooting was avoided. And Father, she thought, as the eldest, was the one who could least endure being arrested.

Here you must forgive me a little sidestep.

How strange it is that such a thing could happen in our parents' small bedroom. I am sure you remember the picture above their bed bidding us a "Good Morning" every day. The picture was of a seven-or-eight-year-old boy of noble birth being questioned by one of Cromwell's brutal soldiers. Frightened weeping ladies in the background. We are told that the boy lied to the soldiers to cover his father's flight from his enemies. I remember how I tried not to look at the picture. It was so frightening and sad. Maybe it had, in a way, an educational effect on us.

The Germans ransacked the whole apartment completely. Cupboards and drawers were emptied and their contents flung on the floor in a general mess. Compromising material was found. Mother had already tidied up. I did admire her enormous calm.

Father had gone to try to establish contact and bring some help for you. It was in the end through my acquaintance with Johan Gjerde that I got into contact with a Nazi police inspector at Møllergaten 19, known as a man one could talk to.

In view of the situation, all odds were against me. I did not have much I could use in your defense. I pleaded that you had had lung diseases, and were somewhat half-witted after being run over as a child. I referred to the scar on your face. Please forgive me. It was not easy for me to lie, but I managed to get a contact from outside Mollergaten 19, which was the whole idea. The police inspector eventually called some people, and the Gestapo, who were now dealing with you, wanted to see me right away. I was to stay at home. The Nazi inspector sent me on my way with the familiar words "Behind the clouds the sky is always blue," and I remember I looked out the window and saw the clouds moving swiftly over the rooftops, now and then revealing a small patch of blue sky. It is funny how you remember details.

I had met Father at Stortorget. He had not been to his office and was more or less hiding. He was in a bad way—he had been waiting for me there for several hours. He had only reluctantly agreed that I should go to the police, and was genuinely afraid that we both, son and daughter, would end up being arrested.

I cannot remember whether it took one or several days before I got the message from Gestapo to go to Viktoria Terrasse and bring clean clothes for you. Whom I was to ask for was rather unclear, but we seized the opportunity. I must have been here at Stokkeli, because I remember I put on my best dress and hat, and took the bag made out of my old flowered curtain, hoping that it would help me a bit. Remember everything had been rationed for quite some time, and I had also grown.

A slope leads up to Viktoria Terasse. It is the steepest and the heaviest slope I can remember ever having walked. I cursed myself for not having been a better student of German in school. This was now a matter of your life and freedom, and all I could do was to stutter and stammer and search for my words.

I repeated to myself what I was going to say. I thought about other times during childhood when I had defended you. When I saved you from the headmaster's wrath—you had curtsied to the teacher instead of bowing. At that time you ran home to Mother as fast as your legs could carry you.

It was easy to get through the enormous, heavy doors at Viktoria Terrasse. Getting *in* was no problem. The reception area seemed big . . . a staircase leading upstairs to the left and another long corridor to the right. Reception desk straight ahead. I went forward with as much calm and self-assurance as I could muster. The guard was the devil himself. Never have I seen a face with such an expression of evil or such wild, fanatical eyes. They actually shone yellow, although they were dark brown. Horror seemed to encompass him, and I had the impression of having entered a dark, black room. The air seemed thick and heavy, as during a fire. I think I could call it the *aura*.

I was to sit down on a bench near the staircase and wait. I waited for a long time. I sat there in all my finery, with an amiable Judas smile, concentrating all of my willpower so that this man should let me go up and see you, while at the same time I despised and hated this representative of the Third Reich. Twice I saw him in action. An explosion of screams and gesticulations calling other guards. First a group of Norwegians came in to ask after prisoners. They were arrested and taken down the corridor to the right. The same thing happened to a couple. They asked their questions and then tried to leave through the main entrance. A struggle ensued. I was sitting there with my false smile. It was terrible.

Then they told me to go up to room so-and-so. It was empty. The door opened and you came ambling in behind another man. You stopped dead when you saw me. Your

back to the door, the bewildered expression in your eyes
betrayed your apparent calm.

I thought you had grown a lot. You were so tall—but later
I realized it was thin you had become. Your hair was dirty
and fell into your eyes. You tried to push it away, but you
stopped and straightened yourself. The man, a Norwegian
Nazi, was a lot older than I. I recognized his face. He used to
live in our neighborhood. He was a very good-looking man
with a rather weak face. He sat down at a desk by the window.

We stood in the middle of the floor, facing each other—
five to six feet apart.

My brother, a prisoner . . . defenseless in the hands of
these people. Of course I knew this was the reason for my
being there. But it was so overpowering to see you, dear
brother, like this. Here in the Gestapo headquarters—how
could I help you? What could I say and what should I do not
to make matters worse? I let all my love and willpower flow
out to you to try to comfort you.

What did I, a young person brought up in secure sur-
roundings in a rather rosy West End, in a peaceful democ-
racy, know about violence and brutality?

I explained I had come with a change of clothing for you.

The moment of eternity ended. Time moved on once
more.

Your reaction was to ask for a comb. A comb. A comb at
such a time.

You straightened yourself up again, like some soldier, and
asked permission to comb yourself. Strange behavior. I
understood that one had to be careful. I did not give you the
comb until the Nazi nodded. You combed your hair. Some
hair fell out and some got stuck in the comb. You were just
going to throw it on the floor, then snapped as if under command, and asked permission to throw it in the stove.

The Nazi had all of this time regarded us intensely. I had a letter for him describing your poor health, making things look very black, signed by a doctor at Grensen. The Nazi got up, took the parcel and the letters, and went into the adjoining room, leaving the door open while he answered the phone.

Maybe he was a little bit moved or really thought we were underlings. It gave me a chance to pretend to brush hair off your sweater. But we embraced, and I whispered, "Hold out, Arne, there's an invasion coming in Europe. In three months everything will be over."

And you replied, "I know."

You knew in spite of being in solitary confinement. The news, fresh from London, obtained by illegal means.

I do not remember whether you were led away first. The meeting was over. It did not actually last many minutes. It was just an interlude. It seemed to have lasted for years. It was impossible there and then to achieve anything. I did not know what you had gone through, interrogations and beatings. You later mentioned that your whole back was black from being beaten, and that you had difficulties walking. That you were so worried that I had also been arrested and become mixed up in all this.

Your childhood friends had been executed the day before. Whether we had made an impression or not is hard to say. Anyway, our file disappeared. And I later got the information that Police General Redeiss left you and your papers behind because of a party he suddenly had to go to. And the executions were over this time around. In this way your life was saved.

I rushed for the door, ran down the cold gray stone staircase. Crying and not giving a damn about it. Almost ran into a Gestapo with a whole case of mackerel. He was shouting out that the mackerel had arrived. The Master Race's mackerel!

I got past the devil himself—the guard at the reception

desk—and ran down the hill and got on the tram, trembling and crying. People sat silently and looked at me. The tram stop was close to Viktoria Terrasse and they instinctively understood.

I was completely overpowered. It was unbearable to leave you alone there. I had to stay in bed for several days.

My thoughts were always with you. You *had* to live, you *had* to become free, you *had* to hold out.

When I sent the half pound of sugar and oats to the long, long prisoner's number, I almost mentally delivered it, like a witch.

We had a happy ending, for which we thank the Lord. And here you are indeed alive, busying the Lord full time to look after you—proving to us and to the world that your eternal optimism is right.

And for that I give thanks.

Sylvei

The roaring westerlies we were surfing on this morning have petered away to a gentle sou'wester. I hate to slow down, but the good news is that the seas are calm enough to let us heave to. If we keep any way up at all, tonight we'll pass the thirteen-hundred-mile mark. We're all ready for a "halfway there" party.

There is something really tight, dry, and cozy about *Tresbelle*'s cabin—the cookstove going, the kerosene lantern swinging, the table dressed out with white, green, and orange hair ribbons, Tone's idea. I make mashed potatoes, corned beef, and onions—Irish enough—all made into a sort of pie and done gratiné (Belsian) and accompanied by carrots and our superb red Bordeaux. Guinness for dessert?

I am absorbed in the meal, but I am impatient to hear from Tone and Chris what they think of Sylvei's letter.

"First off, Bels, you've got a good rock to build your book on," Tone says. "It's very moving . . . memorable. It shows something about the way the two of you got along. It really let me feel as if I were back in 1944, especially that description of

Viktoria Terrasse. Ghosts, maybe, but her reaction helped me feel what living under the Gestapo was really like—how her fears affected the way she saw the building. I know about the terror, of course, but somehow in her letter I could really feel it."

"Yes," Chris agrees. "Imagine the guts that took. What was she, twenty-four? A year younger than Tone. A beautiful young woman going into that jackals' den. To deliver you a comb, Bels . . . all that for a comb. Seriously, it's a very powerful letter."

"As she says, it was only five minutes, but she remembers it in such detail."

"One thing though, Bels," Chris says, "didn't you say that the Stapo arrested you? She says it was the Germans. It may be a small thing, but one inaccuracy spoils reams of good writing."

"Oh, come on," Tone says, "it's not even important. Who gives a damn? She transported me right back there and made me see and feel what it was like. Stapo, Gestapo, who gives a damn?"

"You're right, but still, I know Sylvei, and I really like her, but when I read something I know is wrong it makes me wonder what else is wrong. I'm not trying to be a hard guy, I'm just telling you that's the way it is."

"Her letter showed me just how important those details are," I say. "That one moment stands out for me, too, but I'm trying to write the story of a whole year . . . of all those places, those stories, the different camps, the different trains, guards, dogs, friends. Some of those details run together. Some are just plain gone. Gone for good after forty years. My story can't be much good if the details are all gone."

"They're not, Bels. You can refresh them. You know how things really were. You were there. What made them the way they really were? When you answer that, you've got your story," Chris says.

"Often the best things I write come to me when I'm writing," Tone says. "That's the best stimulus there is."

"I know that's true, Tone. Like Jon," I say. "Now that I'm just thinking seriously about writing, the details about Jon come back to me. I can see his nose, a potato nose almost, just a little turned to the right. His curly chestnut hair. And I see his fingers, long, flat at the tips, strong . . . I can see them playing the piano. You know, maybe the brain never really erases those things. It's sad when I think of them. But telling my friends' story may be a better memorial for them than lighting a candle for them every Christmas."

"You're damn right," Tone agrees. " 'So long as men can breathe or eyes can see / So long lives this, and this gives life to thee.' You're damn right."

"Shakespeare? Shakespeare again, for Christ's sake?"

"Just the party tricks of the overeducated. Am I consigned to the dark ocean air or the serfdom of the galley?"

"Tone, sweet singer, fly you to your rest. Chris and I will clean up. That was beautiful, very beautiful."

Chapter Eleven

Two meters by three . . . my cell is small. The slit windows, the bars, the wooden walls. It feels like a carved coffin. Meeting my sister gave me a jolt of life, of inspiration, but just being in solitary here in Akershus deadens me again. I've been on death row now since I got here. My friends are dead. There is no life, no hope, no heart in any of this. Sylvei and my friends called me an optimist, kidded me about the ridiculously good face that I put on things. There's no good side to this one. There's no silver lining to this cell. I can find life pumping in lots of things. I can see goodness where other people can't find anything but muck, but here it's only muck . . . muck all around.

I kick at the base of the wall, cursing my place and my fate.

"Tssst . . . tssst."

It sounds like a snake. I look around. There's a small hole (a snakehole?) at the base of the wall where it joins the floor.

I've tried that hole looking for contact, for someone to talk to. It's always been dead.

"Tssst. Over here . . . the little hole. Bend down, watch out the guard doesn't see."

We have whispered before down the hallways, but that is hard when there are guards around, which there always are. Who is my new neighbor? I bend down and whisper hello.

"Hello. I'm Professor Tønnesen. I know about you. I'm sorry about your friends."

I knew the Gestapo planted double agents. I knew they might want to talk to me right after my friends had been killed. Maybe they thought they could learn all about our group that way. Maybe that was even why they let me live, I thought. But I also knew about Professor Tønnesen. He had been one of the first people taken when the Nazis encircled the university and began arresting students. The SD wasn't after professors; they were shipping the students off to special camps, trying to draft them into the Waffen SS. Professor Tønnesen had tried to stop the arrests. He had been arrested himself. And here he was in a two-meter-by-three-meter cell. He had been there over six months.

I was a bit cautious talking to him, but before long our "snakehole dialogues" became friendly. He told me everything about the Nazi takeover at the university, about how no one had known how to resist, and about the eleven-hundred students sent to Germany for "indoctrination." "You know these Boches—pardon me, that's an old word from the last war—these Boches really hate scholars and knowledge. Why should they have to convince you if they can just beat you up? Their wonderful 'Aryan purity'—just spend half an hour in a library and you'll find out what tripe they're talking. That's why they put padlocks on libraries as they did at the university."

"What do you teach, Professor?"

"Oh, my subject is Latin. Did you ever study it? That's too bad. But I can teach you. It's a good way to fill the time."

And so it became *amo, amas, amat,* in whispers at all hours of the day through the wall. I had no idea why I would ever want to know Latin, and not even much hope of living long enough to learn it, but it did, indeed, fill the time. As it turned out I did learn it passably well. I wonder if the always devious SD were listening. Could they make anything out of the intelligence that *Gallia est omnis divisa in partes tres?* I felt silly at times, sweating over a dead language. I would rather have been tunneling through the rock to freedom. But Professor Tønnesen was a lively friend. Training my mind on something, even something as remote as Latin, made me feel alive. Then I was transferred.

Grini, ten miles up into the hills behind Oslo, was the main prison for southern Norway. From there I could almost see the island where my parents lived. Built in 1939 as a women's prison, it was now crammed to overflowing with almost eight-thousand prisoners. Around the prison cellblock the Nazis had built clusters of simple one-story barracks. Dangerous prisoners had cells in the main block.

My cellmate had been in the Mil-Org. Because we didn't know each other we didn't talk at all about military things. Life at Grini was better than at Akershus. One day, for example, someone smuggled us four smoked herring—big ones, a foot long. We didn't debate long. Filled with roe, they were fantastic.

I got a smuggled Morse code alphabet, too. Dots and dashes thumped on the bars and walls. We got pretty good. You could send a message almost anywhere in the cellblock.

And then when Schaefchen came on duty as the guard, we had an extraordinary treat. He would give the signal by rapping with his pipe on the table. He was the only one of the

Gestapo I ever met who helped the prisoners. At the end of the war when the Nazis capitulated, the British took good care of him. I heard they actually sent him home to Germany on a special plane as a free man.

When Schaefchen gave the signal, the next thing we'd hear would be the stirring tones of "Sons of Norway" coming out of the air vent. If the coast was then clear there would be a reading of the latest war news over the "system." Hidden in the cellblock was a radio receiver that pulled in the BBC transmissions to Norway. We had all the news every night. One night "Sons of Norway" was interrupted and the "broadcaster" blurted out a message: "The Allies have landed . . . in France. The Allies have landed!"

There were cheers from one end of the prison to the other. "We'll make it! The war will be over in a few weeks! The war is over! They won't kill us now."

But while I was waiting for the war to end, they moved me to Cell 27. I was thrown in with fifteen others. Ragnvald was in the group, thank God. We hadn't been able to talk at all in Akershus, and we'd seemed to miss each other in Grini. His wrinkled brow and constant frown not only were ties with my fast-disappearing past but, as I had begun to see, hid one of the wittiest, most delightful, and most faithful dispositions I have ever found in a friend. Erik, older brother to Dick (alias Stein), my Resistance group leader, was in Cell 27, too. His humor was even zanier, perhaps, than Ragnvald's, and he was more energetic and athletic. He was also a welcome sight. My third friend was Ole. He was taller than I and maybe twice as wide. He looked as though his mother had weaned him and immediately started him chopping wood. There didn't seem to be much hope of pushing the Nazis around, but it still was good to have someone as imposing as Ole in our group.

Most of the others had been living on death row. In Grini we called death row "the parachute." It was a gymnasium stuffed with bunk beds, four levels high, and you needed a parachute to sleep in the upper berths, but the name had even more to do with the "jump" to the other side. Cell 27 was where they gathered "prisoners in transit." Sometimes that meant the "jump," sometimes a transport, most likely to Germany. Our hope was to be moved out to Germany. The farther we got from Viktoria Terrasse the safer we would feel. Who knew when the Gestapo would start another round of executions? And then there were the reprisals. Whenever there was an escape, an assassination, or even a truck blown up, the Gestapo would shoot ten prisoners. That happened a lot to prisoners who survived death row. If they sent us to Germany, they weren't going to ship us back to be shot in a reprisal, we thought.

Our first night in Cell 27 we had a tremendous dinner. Poached cod. A whole case of it. It was very fresh. You couldn't eat it with your spoon because it crumbled into pieces. There were sixteen of us. We were worried. Was this our last supper? Had the boys in the kitchen heard about our fate and sent us in the best they could find? The worry didn't stop us from feasting, from picking up every morsel with our fingers. We had hardly finished licking them clean when we were loaded onto a bus.

Down to Oslo, a night as "guests" at dear old Akershus, and then we were bused back to Grini. The Allies had dropped mines in the Skagerrak, between Norway and Denmark, so no ships were leaving for Germany until the mines were swept clear. I was lucky. Instead of going back into Cell 27, I was allowed out into the barracks. As was true of so many things that happened, I never knew why, but I accepted my good luck. In the barracks the guards were not Gestapo. They were regular German policemen. Often they would say, "I'm going to take a snooze now. Don't run away." Nobody did. The only escapes that I knew of from Grini were when the London headquarters ordered important Resistance people, ones who knew enough to compromise whole units, to escape. The understanding was that they were to escape or die trying. From

London's point of view the result was the same.

We were bused to Oslo again. This time there was a ship. Since sailing to Sweden on the *Mohawk* I'd dreamed of going to sea, but not in the hold of a troop ship bound for a concentration camp in Germany. It was hot and stale in the hold. Finally, after we'd spent ten or twelve hours below, the guards took us on deck.

It was nighttime. There was mist in the air, a breeze from the south or southeast, no stars, but off to port there were lights. A diamond pendant, I thought: along the horizon were strung solitary white, green, and gold beads of light, each one haloed in the salt air. Abeam was a shimmering, reddish-white blaze. It had to be be Göteborg. Neutral Sweden. No blackouts, no Nazis, no concentration camps. Freedom. Freedom shining on the other side of a few miles of black water.

I'd been offshore. I'd told myself, looking in at a coastline, "If I had to, I could swim it." Cold water. Currents. Could I swim it? The war was almost over. There were ten-thousand Norwegians already in Sachsenhausen. The more I debated, the less attractive making the leap seemed. The vision of freedom shining in the night was sweet, but not sweet enough to make me grab at such thin odds.

It was cold on deck. We went below. In Sweden they ate chocolate with every meal, I remembered.

On our third morning aboard we left the Baltic, entered industrialized Stettin Bay, and finally docked behind a coal carrier in the port of Stettin. The trains were at the quay and we marched aboard. Not, however, before Erik managed to don the black cravat that he had gotten who knows where "for our solemn entry onto German soil." I remember feeling something akin to what Sylvei felt looking up at the doors of Viktoria Terrasse—it might be easy to get *in*, but . . .

We had guards, but the train was a regular train, made for people, not for cattle. We rolled, stop and go, for about five hours before we began to wonder. Shouldn't we be seeing Berlin? Wasn't Sachsenhausen near Berlin? We'd passed it. Uh-oh!

Prisoners at the Sachsenhausen *Konzentrationslager* enjoyed Red Cross parcels, letters, food. They didn't have to shave their heads. Health was supposed to be good. The mortality rate was low. But we weren't going there.

Ragnvald had traveled in Germany. He thought he recognized some of the towns, but in the end he only added to our confusion. That first night the train pulled onto a siding near Halle. (I know now that Halle is near the middle of Germany and close to Leipzig.)

In the morning there were sirens and bombs. Concussions blew out windows, and the rail car jumped up and down like a boat. The train next to ours was burning. Our guards fled. There was the smell of burning rubber and dust, dust swirled all through the blistering railyard by the bombs. The smoke and the dust made morning almost as dark as night.

We sat and watched and cheered. We could have been killed, but these bombs were meant for Germans . . . and the war would be over in a week, and it could never happen to us. We all began to notice fluttering debris. Parts of a plane? A barrage balloon? No, it was pieces of light metal, shiny. We didn't know then about using foil strips to baffle radar, but the B-17 pilots most definitely did.

It might have been my imagination, but the guards looked sheepish when they brought us our bread and just a fist-sized chunk of cheese. We might have escaped when they ran to save themselves. But why risk it? Who knew how to get around in Germany? And the war would be over in weeks, you could count on it.

We started rolling right after the raid, our introduction to the wonderful accuracy of daylight bombing. The Allies were definitely winning the war. We rolled on and on. Sometimes we'd be on a siding for an hour or so, but most of that day we traveled. Toward dusk we came to a city. We rolled through it for what must have been half an hour at least. During that whole time we didn't see a single undamaged building. The piles of rubble in most places were higher than what was left standing. We saw people here and there, but no children. No stores with windows, no buildings unscathed. "That was Mannheim," someone said, and it sounded like an epitaph. How could anyone, even the Germans, go on fighting? There wouldn't be anything left of the country. Nothing to live in or fight over. How could the war not be ended in weeks?

The next day we crossed the Rhine. Where the hell were they taking us? On past Strasbourg—"Isn't this in France?"—and into the hills and finally the mountains, the Vosges. The train stopped next at the little Alsatian town of Schirmeck.

Chapter Twelve

chirmeck?"

I'd never heard of Schirmeck.

"Are we still in Germany?"

"We passed Strasbourg. I think we're in the Alsace," said Ragnvald.

"*Los, los!*" New guards, more excited guards, more intense guards. They ranged us into five-man files, shoulder to shoulder. "*Schnell!*" There were four of them and two dogs.

"They must have done this before," Ragnvald observed.

From Schirmeck in the valley we marched up the mountain. We hadn't had food for almost a day. We hadn't been off our train since Stettin. My legs were wobbling. We had trouble keeping the file straight. The guards were SS. They all carried rifles on their backs. Two handled the dogs. Two carried three-foot swagger sticks. Poking, jabbing, kicking at our ankles, they formed us up straighter.

A dog snarled past us and then snapped at Ole Fossum, the

tallest and strongest among us. Ole broke rank slightly. He broke step with the biting, yapping, dog tugging at his calf. He broke step and the guard hit him across the face. It was an easy, backhand motion with his swagger stick, a practiced cut across the nose that brought tears to my eyes just to see. Stung in the face, a dog still at his ankles, Ole was not ready for the straight jab the guard gave him under his ribs. Take the biggest guy, put him up front where everyone else can watch you break him down and humiliate him . . . it must be a noble and wonderful calling to be a prison guard. "March or you will crawl," the scum said in German. March? What the hell else did the bastard think we were doing?

The rough stone road wound up the mountain. We marched up it, but now it was double-time. I was scared to look any-place other than straight ahead, but at each turn you could see out into the valley and across to the far mountains. The trees were big, the country was very diferent from Norway. My island in Oslofjord seemed very far away, but it was pretty country here—mountain country.

Steep grade . . . shaking legs . . . drawing for breath; counting off. "*ein, zwei, drei, vier, fünf.*"

"I'm glad . . . I decided . . . to travel light," Ragnvald said. How could he keep up this pace with his leg? He hardly seemed to be limping.

"How's the leg doing?"

"Terror makes . . . it seem . . . just fine."

I couldn't tell if he laughed.

There was obviously no need to double-time up the moun-tain. It had to be part of the SS *Willkommen*. To show us life would be tough, to break us. Well, dammit, they'd picked the wrong guys to break. Dogsled drivers, mountain guys. Shit, we could go to the top of this mountain . . . and . . . and . . .

"Should've stayed . . . in Akershus," said Erik, and I laughed with the little bit of breath I had left. We came abruptly on some houses. More of a farm settlement than a village, really. But strung around with barbed wire. Was this it? Was this the amp? But we marched on through and still farther up the mountain. "Struthof," the sign said. Struthof. We hadn't yet heard of the gas chamber at Struthof.

Sun, sweat, thin rasps in our throats; no one wanted to break rank. I had settled into the long-distance runner's trance, the rhythm of one foot up, one down, the controlling and husbanding of air and energy, the reluctance even to wipe the sweat from my face for fear it would break the cycle of motion that was keeping me going. I don't know how much thinner the air got as we got higher, but in my mind I knew about it, and in my legs I could feel less and less resilience, less and less capacity to adjust to the rocks and ruts under my feet.

"Next week . . . Bislet . . . for sure."

Ragnvald gave me such a sour look that I decided maybe that hadn't been a particularly inspiring thing to say.

"Next week . . . is pretty . . . far off," he finally answered. About all we could do to keep each other going was sing out with the goddam "ein, zwei, drei, vier, fünf." The bastards had us coming, going, and in between. Maybe one of their goddamn dogs would get heat prostration.

Jogging around the next turn, we saw the camp. Neat, built on terraces, wooden barracks, a chimney. It was almost in the clouds, a good thousand feet farther up the mountain. The cramps in my side had come and gone. I felt I could climb all day. The sled driver was master of the mountains. Maybe this wouldn't be so bad. Maybe this would be a mountain retreat like Grini. We could hide here until the war was over.

Just before we got to camp we passed a prisoner and a guard. The image is familar now, the scarecrow look, the sunken face, the dead eyes, but we had never seen a concentration camp prisoner before.

"Welcome to hell, boys," he said in Norwegian. "They've killed a lot of us."

Through gates and into a dirt quadrangle, gasping, lightheaded, and wobbling from exhaustion. We'd made it.

"Achtung!" Almost before all sixteen of us had arrived, the

call came to fall in. *"Schnell, dummer Norweger! Los! Los!"*
We were locked in our ranks again—rows of five—in the open
space in front of the barracks. They kept us standing at atten
tion in the sun, for what seemed like an hour. Whether it wa
ten minutes or sixty, it gave us time to look around. That wa
when I noticed the gallows.

"Schnell!" Down the little hill in front of us. Guards yelled
at us, and prisoners, too, as we marched. We didn't under
stand, but we hurried anyway. We made up ranks again at the
bottom of the slope. I was in the first file. A guard grabbed
me. With a pair of shears he snipped and slit my traveling
clothes into a pile at my feet. I stood there naked while the rest
of my group were shorn. It was done without comment or
explanation. It was alarming. "So this is how they'll kill us
After bringing us all of this way?"

"Schnell! Los, los!"

Naked, fumbling, groping about for some small piece of
dignity, we were prodded around the corner and into a dimly
lit room.

"Well, they can kill us, but they can't eat us," Ragnvald
said. "It's against the Geneva Convention."

I don't know why I laughed. I had no idea what the SS had
in store for us. In the room we were X-rayed. Chest X-rays
We were quite impressed by the SS's concern for our health
From what we learned later, they were probably worried about
tuberculosis infecting the camp, but we weren't sure, standing
there waiting our turn, just what the machine was for.

"Maybe they think we have guns up our asses," whispered
Erik.

Then they shaved us. The barber was a young prisoner
Dutch, I think. Quickly but surprisingly gently he lopped off
my hair and then shaved my skull to the skin. Armpits, crotch
balls . . . I was glad I didn't have much hair on my chest
Naked, shaven, scared, I was pushed into the pool. The
delousing solution smelled like creosote cut with baby vomit

They shoved me under, let me up, ordered me out—"*Los, os!*"—and gave me new clothes . . . the striped prison uniform of the *Vernichtungslager* and *Konzentrationslager*. These moderately heavy "pajamas" (too warm for summer, not warm enough in winter) were made of heavy cotton or ersatz cotton, grayish blue with dark blue stripes. They were not brand new, but they wear well," Erik said. Painted in red on the back of the uniforms were the letters NN. This is Natzweiler. Natzweiler Norweger?

Five minutes, maybe six. That's all it took. Stripped, X-rayed, shaven, and deloused. None of us knew what it might mean. Erik, Ole, and I were standing to one side of the delousing area. "Natzweiler?"

"What kind of camp is it?"

"I've never heard of it."

"Do you suppose they don't feed you at all? That guy outside looked like death."

The sixteen of us were standing there, talking for the first time since Schirmeck, no guards in sight, when a prisoner, wearing the same stripped pajamas we'd just received, strode up to us and started barking some weird and unintelligible orders. I cut through his accent to make out that he was speaking German. Who was this guy? Christ, we had enough people telling us what to do without high and mighty prisoners bossing us around.

I'm not sure what the man said, but I told him, "Heil Hitler yourself, you *Schmendrik*." I casually turned away, to let him shrivel under my insult.

"Arne!"

I heard the warning shout in time to scissor aside so that his foot plowed into my thigh instead of shattering my knee. Why hadn't I noticed? None of *us* had boots. There was quite a fuss. That's how we learned about capos.

Capos—the prisoners whom the Germans put in power in the camps, the criminals who were allowed total freedom over

the other prisoners. Mostly German criminals, occasionally
"the chosen" from other nationalities, capos were the sickest
cogs in the demented system of the German *Konzentrationslager*. Each block had a capo leader, each barracks had a capo
chief. Behind the fences, under the protection of the guards,
these capos managed the day-to-day affairs of the prisoners.
They had life-and-death authority. They ruled by intimidation
and bullying. Sometimes they were even given quotas, told to
eliminate a number of us. It was beautifully orchestrated: the
Nazis kept clear of "prison filth" while the capos did their bru-
talization for them. Power corrupts . . . and the Nazis put
power in the hands of the already corrupted. That sort of brilliant management made their system of "solutions" work ter-
rifyingly well.

"*Achtung!*" the head guard called from the top of the hill.
"Up, up, faster, faster!" We were harried back from the "baths."
We formed ranks and once again waited in the sun.

Out of the administration building, flanked by guards and
two huge capos, came the commandant. He looked the part.
He was in his fifties, and the only thing to detract from his
Teutonic ferocity and Aryan lordliness was a noticeable double chin.

"*Willkommen. Willkommen in Natzweiler, Vernichtungslager Natzweiler*," he began in clear, level tones. "Natzweiler
is not a *Konzentrationslager*, not a concentration camp. It is a
Vernichtungslager, a destruction camp."

He warmed up. "For the protection and purification of the
Reich, the need is clear. There are lice and ticks and weevils
that would threaten the health of the Reich. There are enemies and misfits who threaten the order. *You* are enemies and
misfits. Sons of whores, *You* are the pitiful lice, the slimy weevils, who threaten the Reich. You have been brought here to
be eliminated . . . squashed, crushed, like the bugs that you
are. Here you will be dealt with . . . exterminated!"

He delivered all of that almost without taking a breath, or
so it seemed. His voice had risen now to a shout. It went up

and down for emphasis, but it stayed at the same loudness. It was hard for me to understand, and I was happy that I didn't, but here is what I think I heard:

"This is not a threat. To stamp you out is not a promise, even. It is a fact. You are dead. You have already died. You are . . . you are . . . the *already dead.*" He laughed. "You are mysterious, marvelous, living dead . . . you are"—and I couldn't believe his voice could go louder, but it did—"ALREADY DEAD."

"Those red letters on your backs. Those letters set you apart. You are NN, you are anonymous, you are *Nacht und Nebel,* you are ALREADY DEAD! Next to your number there is no name . . . a number only. Only the living have names. You are anonymous . . . *Nacht und Nebel.* You used to crawl and slide and creep in the night and fog, *Nacht und Nebel.* We crush you, swat you, exterminate you into *Nacht und Nebel,* the night of the noose, the fog of the crematorium.

"No one in the world knows where you are, and, *Unter-menschen,* you will not long be in this world. Disappear, you little gnomes, disappear!" He shook his fist in front of his red-dened face. Spittle flecked both corners of his mouth. His eyes were brown-and-white beans jumping behind the steamy lenses of his thick glasses. He shook his fist at us and then pointed. Our heads turned to the foot of the compound. He was pointing at the crematorium. It was a squat building, above it lanced a brutal-looking steel chimney. "You have come home, scum. This"—and he poked his finger excitedly toward the crematorium—" this is your home. *Willkommen,* already dead! *Welcome to Natzweiler.*"

I couldn't believe it. I couldn't believe any of it . . . that I was on some mountaintop in the Vosges, that they could do this to me, to us, to anyone, that anyone, even an SD commandant, could walk out into the sunshine of a summer afternoon and tell people they were already dead. I couldn't believe Herr Kommandant could bellow and rant for almost an hour.

From the frightening things he said, I realized that we were

really in for it. But how could he take himself seriously? Another
hollow man. That was the thing with the Germans; they all
took themselves so seriously. It was either terrifying or absurd
. . . or both. No name, no future, no hope . . . witness to my
own absence, a number with no name. A nightmare with no
waking up. How could they stand here with cities flattened all
around them, the Wehrmacht being pushed back from the
fortress wall, the country bleeding to death, and talk about the
already dead? Christ, it was too strange.

But we could hold on. We could stay undead until all of
their goddam cities were parking lots. We could stay on the
living side of that crematorium until Allied tanks came clanking up this mountain. We could keep alive until the Mosquito
bombers were buzzing around that fucking chimney. We could
hold out . . . so long as one of those shit-smelling capos didn't
kill us with a rock or take us out on a last work detail.

In the barracks we talked for the first time to prisoners who
had been in the camp awhile. And we finally got a meal—an
inch-thick slice of heavy rye bread and a bowl of imitation
coffee. The prisoners talked, most in flat, lifeless voices, of
who had come here, and who had died. The lists were almost
equal. Norway is like a single village. We all knew someone.
They asked about life back home. Their eyes seemed to be
staring into a fire. I wondered if "home" existed anymore, for
them, for us. I tried pretending that Natzweiler didn't exist.
They told us about the capos and how to live with them, about
the work and the Appellplatz. We listened because we had to,
to stay alive, but we hardly wanted to hear.

I loved these men. They were brothers, they were Norwegians, they were heroes. But I shied away from them—I didn't
like to admit it. I didn't like this distance, but I put it there,
blocked them off to save myself—not so much from them as
from their death disease. Because even I could see that these
prisoners were already dead.

Chapter Thirteen

From Herr Kommandant we got the Natzweiler welcome. From the capos we get the Natzweiler program: "We wash you, then we kill you." We had already been washed.

Work at Natzweiler was quarrying. It was brutal work made more so by senselessness. Prisoners carried rocks to the bottom of the hill, broke them into stones, then carted them back up. All day, every day. But there wasn't enough room in the quarry (nor on the gallows) for all of us. So we were treated to the *Appellplatz*.

They held roll call and assembly at Natzweiler on terraces directly below the gallows. They had no work for us, so we were drilled on the *Appellplatz* twice and sometimes three times a day. There were many days when we never left it. Roll call and counting—*ein, zwei, drei, vier, fünf*—went in rows of five. They would count us. They would count us and count us again. If there had been an escape they would spend the whole day counting us, *ein, zwei, drei, vier, fünf,* over and over and over again. They started this at five in the morning. Sometimes we were there after dark.

All during the counting we stood at attention. No one wanted to be caught breaking ranks. Capos lived for the joy of humiliating someone who broke ranks. Yelling in your face from an inch away was just the beginning. No matter how prepared you were, no matter how long you'd been around and seen this silly game, the capos always seemed able to find a new way to hurt you. They were brutal and sneaky and bored, and they devoted themselves to making us look and feel bad so that they would look good in front of the guards. You'd think a capo was raising his foot to stomp on your toe and then feel the lightning agony of his knee to your balls or his palm flat under your chin. For troops in peak physical condition the *Appell*, the roll call, would be strenuous. For people living on cabbage-water soup, a bowl of coffee, and a slice of bread, the strain could be fatal.

During my second or third *Appell* I noticed prisoners around me taking their caps off; they uncovered one by one. Pretty soon I was the only one in my sector with a prison beret still on my head. I saw then that some capos were passing with a stretcher. The blue look and rolled eyes of the prisoner made it obvious. He had died in the ranks.

The whole incident had a strange effect on me. I saw the man's unshaven face, shaved skull, and brown-stained teeth in my mind's eye for days afterward. I had not seen death before. I didn't know this prisoner at all. I wondered why his death's-head face was so hard for me to forget. Could it have been my confusion over the cap salute? Could it be that because I didn't pay my respects, didn't "bury" him properly, the prisoner continued to haunt me? Through generations of civilization we've developed rituals to protect ourselves; is this what happens when you don't observe them? If I'd doffed my cap would I still see the man's last grimace, even today? I still don't have the answer, but there were other questions. How far would our captors go to break us, for instance.

We were summoned to the *Appellplatz* to watch hangings and public beatings. The punishment for stealing food, for instance was twenty-five lashes. That amounted to a death sentence when your skin and bones were as close together as most of ours. In Konzentrationslager Natzweiler the first hanging I saw was botched; the knot was badly adjusted so it let the prisoner fall so far his feet were touching the ground. The SS guard dug a hole in the gravel with the toe of his boot to let the spasming victim hang.

The barracks are where we spend what's left of our time. One-story sheds perhaps thirty meters long, they are jammed with all the bunk beds that will fit, three tiers high. The bunks aren't private—there are a minimum of two prisoners per bunk. Sometimes I've slept with three others. When one moves, everyone moves. There is a washroom with cold water and then the toilets: open rows of stools. The stink of sickly shit and dysentery is thick everywhere. You get used to it enough so that you can breath out by the bunks, but when you have to go to the toilet it's suffocating. Almost as much as the work, the lack of food; and the disease, it wears away at us.

We try to stick together. Ragnvald and I sleep in the same bunk when we can. It is better than shivering through the chill mountain nights. Erik has just been talking to a French prisoner.

"He said Bull killed two people today, grabbed two prisoners by the neck and beat their heads together. He was standing down in the quarry. My friend says he almost threw a rock down on him, but *il ya des autres méthodes de se suicider*"— there are other ways of committing suicide.

Bull is the worst of the capos. Every day there's a story about him. Everyone avoids him, because he's known for rages, for flying into a tantrum and crushing the closest person to hand. But at least he's predictable. Some of the sneakier ones seem even worse to me.

Tore Hytten, a Norwegian from Kragerø, was here when we arrived. He says to Ragnvald, "We might as well all commit suicide if we don't get anything else to eat. Up here in the mountains there isn't anything but rocks. They won't give us anything, we can't find anything. You'll see, Natzweiler means 'nothing to eat.' There just *is* nothing to eat."

Ragnvald looks at me slyly. I nod. "Tore," he says, "we've got something for you." He reaches beneath the bed for his steel *Schüssel*, his bowl. He hands Tore a glob of something from it. The rest of the group turn shoulders outward to make a circle shielding Ragnvald and Tore from the surrounding prisoners.

"Coffee grounds? Surrogate-coffee grounds?"

"Well," says Regnvald, "you can talk about eating or you can eat."

"Well, this isn't food. There's no—"

"Tore," Ragnvald says, "you certainly don't have to take any. Arne and I risked our asses during breakfast to be the first ones to the back of the kitchen. We got there in time to get some, and we're going to eat some more. Just thought you might like to see what a full stomach feels like."

"Okay, I'll try some."

Ole, at the foot of our stack of beds, doesn't seem to notice the "picnic" going on next to him. Finally he gets up and goes to the toilet.

"He is in trouble," says Tore.

"He's been that way since we got off the ship. He's all curled up in a shell. Nothing touches him. I envy him that, but he's just shriveling up. What the hell's wrong with the guy? He's the strongest one of all of us," says Ragnvald.

"Physical strength has nothing to do with it," says Tore. "Or maybe it does, but only because he's used to relying on muscles that have dried up on him, have shrunk up like his stomach. Maybe that's why he's so depressed."

"I don't know what we can do. He looks like he's given up," I say.

"There was a guy in our group just like that," Tore says. "Turns out he was waiting to make an escape."

"Maybe so," I say. "Around home Ole was a leader. You can tell how strong he was. He used to have a lot of muscle on those big bones. Maybe you're right. Maybe losing his strength sapped Ole more because he had more to lose. When we got here the guards picked on him because he looked so tough compared to the rest of us shrimps. They must know something. They leave him alone now. Do you think he's playing that game? Lying low? Or do you think it's just that you have to be a bit of a jerk to laugh in this place? Maybe he's too honest to say 'It'll never happen to me.' Maybe he just recognizes what's happening to all of us, what's bound to happen to all of us. Maybe he's just a realist," says Erik.

"Piss off, Erik," Ragnvald says, only halfjoking.

"Where's your goddam tie? With that kind of philosophy you ought to be using it to hang yourself," I add.

"That's it, you assholes, that's the way we should stick together. That's real inspiring," Erik answers.

"Just the same, I worry about him," Tore says.

There's a scuffling in the corner. We hear the high, excited voice of Hermann, the *Blockälteste*, the capo in charge of the barracks. It is normal for him to be ranting, kicking, whipping his way around the barracks about now. We don't pay much mind until Erik says, "Oh, my God."

We look.

Hermann has piled about fifteen prisoners into a heap in the corner. He has unlimbered his leather whip. He is laying it out and snapping it over their heads. As they cower he starts to croon, *"Schweine, Schweine."* He says it in a strange, singsong way that is somehow different from normal cursing. He begins laying the lash into the pile of people. It is a mixed bag of prisoners. What the hell did they do? I've never seen this before.

He is good with the whip. No one can slip out from under it. The pace of his shouts is quicker, sharper. The lash keeps time. I've never seen this.

Lashes and *Schweine,* faster and faster. Hermann's eyes glaze; he's gasping now, panting. I realize I am watching the capo quite literally "whipping himself off." There is an empty circle of floor around Hermann. He jerks and whips and quivers to his climax. He shudders, whip withdrawn and drooped to his side, then lurches across the floor to a table. He leans heavily on both hands for a long, silent, awkward time. He looks around . . . challenging, reveling, smirking. The prisoners don't know what to do, how to get away. Some have welts on arms and necks. Cowed, ashamed, we sit and wonder what to do while Hermann cleans his front with his shirttail. I wonder how Hermann got his kicks before the war.

Roll call, "spectacles," and drills, all happened on the *Appellplatz.* The drills were senseless, a sort of parody of German army drill. All of this suffering, these guards, these fences and dogs, whips and guns, gallows and crematoria, and the end result is . . . "Vee can make zem take zayre caps off." The drills were built around the five-man ranks, the *ein, zwei, drei, vier, fünf* of the roll call. Incredible time was devoted to "dressing ranks," getting our lines straight enough to satisfy the capo field marshals. No matter if we were in drill-team perfection, they hit us anyway. There was no point to the drill, particularly. It just went on and on, capos and swagger sticks and whips and standing and shouting. "*Mützen ab!*"—Caps off! "*Mützen auf!*"—Caps on! through interminable July afternoons. "*Augen rechts!*"—Eyes right! *Die Augen links!*—Eyes left! It was interesting to see how perfectly suited is the German language for giving commands. *Die* with *Augen* told us, before we even heard the directional command, that *links*, left, would follow, but *Augen* alone was invariably followed by *rechts*, right. Precision is built into the grammar. We might have achieved drill-team perfection if we'd cared to. The structure of the language solved the problem of left versus right, solved the problem of perfect anticipation and obedience. This experience helped me understand the German record of military precision and tendency to use it.

But the big question wasn't one of confusing left and right or of being out of sync. It was mental and physical endurance. The rattle and thud of death in the ranks was a daily thing on the *Appellplatz*. The stretcher bearers were on hand all the time.

One glorious August afternoon, drill ended early. We were ranged in the shade of the barracks. There was a disturbance by the gate. Across the camp, on the other side of the *Appellplatz*, we saw a group of guards. Moving at the center of the guards were people . . . young people . . . women. Four women.

They were far away. We could see that they were young. I saw them waving, making V signs to us. We waved back. We wished they were closer. I couldn't tell much about their faces, but they were young, attractive.

"English," came the word, almost before they'd disappeared down the steps and into the crematorium. I was reminded of watching my friends dragged off down the sunlit passageway at Akershus. Now the women were locked up down in the crematorium. English? I wondered how English women had gotten to this mountaintop in the Alsace. Women in civilian clothes, young women, pretty women. It was certain that it was not a happy thing for them to be at Natzweiler.

"Oh shit, no!" I was sitting on a bunk in the barracks when Erik told me.

"They've hanged the women. Two English, two French. They were in uniform when the Nazis caught them, the pricks."

I walked into the lavatory, just to walk away. The stink, the stink of it all, got to the back of my throat, and I vomited up my cabbage water and bread. Those women had been full of life, and for a minute they had pricked through the protective crust on my soul.

Nacht und nebel was a "special status" in the Nazi view of things. There were only a few other NN camps besides Natzweiler—Ravensbrück and Mauthausen, for example. All told there were about five thousand NN prisoners. There were 504 Norwegians. I was among the youngest.

I found it interesting to read after the war that Hitler's *Nacht und Nebel Erlass*, a decree establishing the quaint category of NN prisoners, was issued on December 7, 1941, the same day the Japanese attacked Pearl Harbor. The idea of the NN classification was that death was not enough to break resistance movements. A greater deterrent was needed. What Hitler ordered was that NN prisoners disappear without a trace, that no kind of information be provided about their whereabouts or fate. Evidently Hitler felt that such disappearances would paralyze potential resistance. Certainly public executions have sometimes worked to incite it.

I wonder if Sylvei had been summoned to Viktoria Terrasse because of some thinking like that . . . because they wanted to keep me alive so I could disappear. *Das Rheingold*, the dark prince Alberich, *Nacht und Nebel*, and poof!

Death camps were the final refinement of the Nazi "final solution." It's inspiring how they went from firing squads to exhaust-filled trucks to poison to the gas chamber. Ingenuity triumphs over even the nastiest challenge. When you want to eliminate whole populations you've got to be efficient. To handle the flood of Jews and other "racials" and "undesirables" the Nazis evolved the death camps. Big, automated, organized, they were manned with people who clipped the hair that filled the mattresses, cut the clothes that made the rags, pulled the teeth that contained the gold, got the effects that the "patients" wouldn't need, dispatched the souls, and cremated the bodies (an average of twenty thousand a day at Auschwitz in its prime), and still managed to take most afternoons off.

The NN camps weren't the same thing. Our group was small. They could have shot us all in a day and been done with it. But the purpose of our camps was different. What the SD wanted was a sort of revenge drama, almost a cat-and-mouse torment instead of instant death. After making us disappear, or while doing so, they made sure to extract the gravest penalty possible for our sins. Resistance, you see, was our sin.

I think I am right. Natzweiler was geared not so much to kill us, but to destroy our ability or desire to resist. It was an ongoing antiresistance laboratory. As the SS in particular discovered, killing resisters often breeds new resistance. Everywhere the Reich went, it spawned resistance. Conquer resisters or tame them and that would remove one very significant roadblock to world domination. The commandant at Natzweiler and his SS, SD, and capos were united in twisting us, in stretching us, in stifling us, in trying to achieve that point where we had no will for resistance, no will to resist even death.

We are being counted. The *Appellplatz* show has been going on since sunup. The sun is high. It must still be morning. *Ein, zwei, drei, vier, fünf.* The counting is like a wave of sound running down one side of the place, back up the other. Hoarse and dry, it reminds me of skreeing gulls in the wake of a fishing boat. I imagine an albatross wheeling through mist and moonshine shadowing us.

> *The souls did from their bodies fly—*
> *They fled to bliss or woe!*
> *And every soul it passed me by*
> *Like the whizz of my crossbow.*

Sometimes, when I can get away with it, I use a special *Appell* technique to try to keep body and soul together. To rest. It is a simple matter for someone as tall as I am to cross one leg in front of the other and perch, like a roosting chicken, with the other leg in the hollow above my kneecap. My friends laugh, I laugh, but laughing is good for us. I am sure I've discovered a secret of nature.

"*Ein, zwei, drei, vier, fünf!*"

"*En, to, tre, HAL!*—the big mainsail takes another jump up the mast. Twenty of us pull, twenty strong hands from Norway. Charlie Barr knows to leave us to Sven. Sven counts. We heave."

En, to, tre, HAL!

Atlantic—the big black schooner. Charlie Barr—the America's Cup skipper. The squareheads, twenty-two professional sailors from Stavanger, and Sven, the sailing master. I've read the tales. Now, as I perch on the *Appellplatz*, my mind gifts me with the picture of the black, curving bow of the big schooner as she does fourteen knots across the North Atlantic. Into my empty prisoner's head come ghost impressions, comes the feel of heaving on an inch-thick halyard, comes the sight of an iceberg ruddering the fog, comes the look of Charlie Barr squinting upward, comes a white wake laid like a road over the gray-blue water, come the navigator's numbers: 341 miles in twenty-four hours.

No sailboat ever before went that far that fast!

"*Ein, zwei, drei, vier, fünf!*"

I exchange legs. I think I can recapture my dream of the foggy banks and the big schooner, but something instead steers me to visions of French bread . . . the smell from the bakery, the nearly hard crust, the sound of the bite . . . but no, the tug and pull of ripping the bread apart to prepare for the bite, it is . . .

"*Achtung! Achtung!*"

I see something unusual; purposeful movement makes it way

down the rows in front of me. Maybe someone has died. No hats off, but then there have been so many deaths that we have stopped taking our hats off. No one said anything, no one decreed a rule. We were just worn out. The respects and the trouble to pay them seemed too much. We used to stand in solid tribute to fallen brothers. Now the stretchers come and go without notice.

It must be an air raid I hear. Artillery? Come on. I can't believe it. Have the Allies gotten this far? I look to catch Ragnvald's eye. He's two rows in front of me today. I see that the capos are moving along with some sort of cart. They're moving down the rows with a cart. There's another one to the other side of me. That one looks closer. It really sounds like artillery.

The cart stops and the capos hand something to each row. I wait, I crane and peek (without, of course, breaking ranks). The cart is closer. I see it's filled with tins. Tins? They've come and gone. They gave each row a tin. Meat? Meat! A quarter-pound tin. We're meant to share it. We must be evacuating.

I got a loaf of bread. They gave each prisoner a loaf of bread for the trip. Not French bread, exactly, but this might be an evening when wishes comes true.

In files of five they march us down the mountain. There are capos and dogs everywhere, interspersed with SD and SS. Shouting, barking, whipping, we make a Babel of our retreat. I can still hear the guns. The low honeyed light of the setting sun throws faces into shadow, throws shadows down the trail, and makes a black step-pyramid mass of the terraced compound behind us. Ragnvald, Ole, and I are in one group. We've lost Erik.

"Halt!" Like a topple of dominoes the order ripples up the trail. It strikes me that we have taken the *Appellplatz* show on the road. Skull-shaven, sunken-eyed, pajama-clad shadows fill up the mountainside. I expect that next they'll have us taking off and putting on and eyes right into the sunset. Just behind us there's a capo haranguing the Russians. An SS taps his swagger stick to the capos forehead to order silence. The capos, the Russians, and the SS . . . they truly deserve one another. If one of each were drowning, which would I save first?

About face? What the hell's going on here? Back? To Natzweiler? Squinting into the low sun, we grumble. There's a flare of something that feels like resistance, but there are guns and guards and dogs enough to send us back to camp. Subdued, without even much noise from the dogs, we return. Partisan activity in the woods, they say . . . the advance group heard shots. We're back. What are they going to do now?

I leave Ole and Ragnvald to look for Erik. I try the barracks, the kitchen. Maybe he's looking for me. Next I head into the far barracks. It's empty. I stretch out for a second. I fall asleep.

A slobbering, snarfing sound, like a dog with a plate of scraps, brings me out of my sleep. They don't usually let the dogs run loose, but maybe in the confusion and everything . . .

I shake myself awake and look over the side. Two bunks away is a prisoner. He has opened a tin of meat. He is eating it. The sounds subside, I see him licking at the tin, pouring the last of the gravy onto his tongue. He belches, flat, shuddering belches, then he lies back. He mumbles something to himself. I think he's Russian. I hear him put the tin under the bunk.

Noisily and fast, three other men come in. They look around. The man below me starts to get up. Snarling in Russian, the other three close in on him. There are questions . . . confident answers . . . shouted questions . . . over-confident answers. Then one of the three finds the empty tin. The howl, the screech, then they attack the fourth. He kicks, gurgles, and thrashes. His sphincter lets go and puddles the bunk with one last dose of shit. With a sound like snapping wood shingles, the prisoner rattles, chokes, and dies.

Still moaning laments to one another, the three depart. Cirding wide around the new corpse, I follow close behind. Even the monstrous, grinding routine of the camp seems shattered. I have no idea where my friends are. Should I hide here? It's after dark. How could they find me? I'll just wait here for the Allies. Or wait to be shot when they find me. It's a chance to take. A chance to take with the war about to end? Well, what if the Nazis kill all of us so we can't say what we've seen? The Nazis know no one will believe us.

An SS man came and swept me out of the barracks to the *Appellplatz* to join the five thousand waiting to leave the camp. I am almost thankful to see the jackboots and uniform of some kind of authority in the darkness of this hell that seems to be deepening all around me.

I don't find Erik, but Ole and Ragnvald are where I thought they'd be. We form ranks. Together the shadow people of Natzweiler march into the darkness outside the fence.

It might have been easy to escape on the way down, but the dogs, the whips, and the capos cow us. Holding on to each other to stay in the road, marching under a shroud of curses and noise, we edge down the mountain. The shuffling *klok klok klok* of wooden clogs over gravel, like cracked castanets, is our contribution to the surreal scene. At a turn in the road I looked my last on *Konzentrationslager Natzweiler*. Against the dark slope the crematorium chimney glows cherry red, a pencil of light grimly memorializing the one hundred and fifty that were hanged there on our final day. The obscene spear seems like a portent, but whether it's a swift sword announcing the coming Allies or a fiery poker driving us deeper into Nazi hell I really couldn't say.

Chapter Fourteen

It's perfect spinnaker weather. It's so good we've taken the mainsail down. I love sailing under just the spinnaker. I love looking at the sail, watching it lift, seeing it pull. It's like a sled dog, hard to start but great once you get it pulling.

You can trim the spinnaker and guy it down so it will keep pulling even if the wind shifts twenty or thirty degrees. Seas from astern lift a boat around, but when you've got a spinnaker straining out in front of you, it dampens the motion and smooths the ride. And speeds it up. Spinnakers are fast. The strain on the sheet, the tension on the guy—the boat feels that power and comes alive.

When I sailed in six-meters with Calle right after the war we flew spinnakers every day. We flew them sideways, around stays, around spreaders, around themselves, and around us. We sent spinnaker poles skying, diving, crashing, tearing, and breaking. We put spinnakers up cocked, turned, upside down

twisted, tied in a ball, and knotted. We took them down full
of wind, full of water, snagged and tearing, too late, too early,
and not at all. I had a little trouble with spinnakers. But take
time, take sea room, take a relaxed approach, and spinnakers
can be magic carpets, honeymoon balloons, parachute rides.

Aeolus, the Olympian god of the winds—a nicely drawing
spinnaker always reminds me of Aeolus. "Blow, winds, and
crack your cheeks." *Tresbelle* is making a sedate six knots under
spinnaker alone right for our landfall at Arran Island off the
northwest corner of Ireland.

By the occasional bare knee, shoulder, or buttock that I can
see from the cockpit, it looks like Tone has warmed to the sun.
Beach days don't happen often in the North Atlantic. Tone's
lying on a towel, wearing only sunglasses, reading up on the
foredeck.

Chris has the watch. I'm peeling potatoes over the stern rail.

I laugh. "I'm throwing more food overboard now than I saw
in a week in the camps."

Chris gives me a look. "Jesus, this is too nice a day . . . I'm
sorry, I don't mean to sound like a fool, but it *is* too nice a day
to do anything except feel the sun and listen to the miles click
away."

"You young people have no sense of responsibility. All
escapists. A naked woman on the bow, an easy rider in the
cockpit. Did you see signs for Woodstock out here somewhere?"

"What do you know about Woodstock, Bels? Don't tell
me you were there, swimming nude, diving stoned off the
rocks."

"No, I was at the time the kingpin of several very bourgeois
and revoltingly small businesses in Oslo. You were just a kid,
weren't you?"

"Yeah, about eleven. But I eventually saw the movie.
Woodstock, I mean. I must say it hasn't changed my life. Every
time I go to a concert, though, I feel sort of cheated. After

Woodstock I sort of expect peace, joy, love, and happiness along with the music."

"This kind of day lightens all kinds of burdens."

"Couldn't be better. What's it been—two weeks? Two weeks . . . night and fog and hair-raising disaster. It's nice to come up for air. . . . I'm curious, Bels—were there any pleasant days in the camps, any at all? There had to have been one or two. Did you ever get to come up for air?"

"No."

"I see."

"None at all."

"Uh huh. God, that must have been grim."

"Not so much. It wasn't that there weren't nice situations. Good weather at least, but . . . well, how can I say it? I don't want to sound morbid. I don't want to cry and moan too much, but no, there was no such thing as a good day in the camps.

"Part of it was you were down to such an elemental level that you only reacted to things like food and warmth. I mean, if a woman as pretty as Tone came into the barracks in Dachau naked, most of us wouldn't have had the energy to do more than smile."

"Days like this . . . we didn't have any the last time I crossed. It was earlier in the summer. Days like this are pretty rare and pretty wonderful," Chris says.

"I was feeling too lazy to take a bath, but if we're not going to get another day like this one, maybe I'd better seize the opportunity."

I finished my potatoes and went below. Rooting around for my shaving kit, I thought about the two on deck. Wouldn't they be sunbathing together, making love under the spinnaker, if it weren't for grizzled old me? I wondered how they'd get along. Maybe keeping watches and reefing sails and making meals is the best therapy for old lovers. There's something crackling there, I think. They tease each other, but sometimes the lightness evaporates and I think I see them raking each other. I don't know. Would it spoil anything if they were rolling around on the deck now, gasping and moaning? Would it help anything? Would it spoil something? Is there a boat big enough for Madeleine and me to sail the way Chris and Tone do? Friends. With my spirits lifted like this, with the running and ducking and gritting that I've done since the camps lifted some, would I have been big enough to make it work with Madeleine? Even today under the glorious spinnaker I think of the children, of Gustave so stiff and faraway, of Nic and Catherine who won't acknowledge me at all. Have Chris and Tone put some pieces together, just as it seems? Could I?

Chris has undressed to a bathing suit. The plastic cans of water lashed to the stern rail are sun-warm. I fill my bucket/ basin from them and have a civilized shave. Naked and soaping myself, I hear: "Dolphins!"

"Where?"

"Right under the bow."

Tone stands to look, I crane forward, Chris mans the wheel. We've had dolphins from time to time since we started. Today there are about twenty. They're playing in the bow wave, criss-crossing in our wake, torpedoing in from amidships. I never get tired of dolphins. It amazes me how quickly individuals emerge. You see their faces only for a flash, but they're unique and memorable, like human faces. Rough teeth and long snouts give *Tursiops truncati* its "smile," but what explains how a dolphins smile goes with its eyes? In this group now, there's Bruce, the pretty boy; Zsa Zsa, the nuzzler; Sigurd, grizzled and wise; and Rantas, the raging one.

Close under the bow in the shadow of the spinnaker you can see beneath the water to watch them play. They sense an audience. There were two . . . now there are eight. They play tag, they slow-dance, they boogie, they barrel-roll and then, "Pshawww," they take a breath— "How was that?"

In my next life I'll be a bottlenose dolphin. At the end of this one I'll have my ashes strewn on the sea. Maybe that will help the transition.

We talked this morning with a Canadian weather ship. She

confirmed our position (750 miles to the canal!) and then asked, "Where are you bound?"

"Oslo, Norway," I answered.

"Oh my God," came the reply.

Tonight is Ellen's birthday. I was set for a solitary exercise in depression, but Tone suggested a birthday dinner. Tone always hits things just right. She and Ellen have gotten to be fast friends. I feel a lot better sharing the celebration. I know what I'd like to have for a birthday dinner, though. A fabulous Norwegian salmon. They can be caught! They come from the west coast of Norway, where fjords are deep and chill, where rock and ice and pine and sky are arranged to stop your heart, where snowcapped mountains are there to touch. The one I love in the place that I love, that's my birthday wish for her, and me.

And for dessert some of the famous mountain strawberries in the even more famous local sour cream, thick and tainted with just a sinful trace of sugar. I know just where to get them.

I stow my fantasies and we prepare something for real life. We bustle on and off the helm, each of us taking time to slice, dice, saute, purée, or flame before retaking the con.

The tinned salmon steaks are beautiful. I make up potato salad, and a cream sauce for the canned peas. We have a beautifully iced (grâce â Tone) box cake, and of course a taste more of our estimable Bordeaux. Do you have any idea how well that red Bordeaux goes with salmon? Happy birthday, Ellen.

We hove to eat. There wasn't much wind at the time. Now something feeble from the northeast has materialized. It might keep us going. Hard on the wind, but there isn't much of it, so the seas should stay calm awhile. Chris gallantly goes topside to get us sailing again. Tone and I gallantly stay below in the warmth of the littered galley. We wash well together. It is a fine feeling to hand dripping things to someone who knows where they go.

"How come you're not married, Tone?"

"Is this the beginning of an extremely immodest proposal?"

"You know I have no room in my tangled life, even for a wonderful woman like you. No, I just was thinking how much of the time you must be alone."

"Well, first of all, you don't need to be married just to have a man around. Even a relic like you knows that."

"True enough."

"So I might say: I haven't met the right fellow—patently false. Or that I don't like washing dishes—but look at me now. Or that I love my independence—closer to the truth, but the independence to drive my cab six nights a week in Oslo is a mixed blessing. I don't know, Bels, you tell me."

"Well, it's not because you're a hag."

"Thank you, Sir Gawain. I don't know, Bels. I've been in love, but never in love enough to work at making things work. I mean, they happen, and they're great. They stop happening, and that's it—they're over, it's over, I don't know. I never tried too hard to control all of that. If you want a semiserious answer, though, I guess they key might be in my parents. They stayed together until they died in the fire. I think all children must idealize their parents. It was something about the way they were forged together in my mind by the way they died. I've never gotten over that. I think of them as a unit, and I can't think of them any other way. I'm not ready myself to be a part of something like that. I wonder whether I ever will be."

"I wonder about Ellen."

"We've talked. I think she's different. She talks of it as 'the next step,' and 'an adventure.' I don't think you'll find a lady cabbie on your hands with Ellen."

We go topside. It is sunless, midnight. There is more life in the water than we've seen. It almost sparkles. Maybe we're wandering back toward the Gulf Stream or it's wandering back toward us, but the water is shot with phosphorus. Here and there blue bullets shoot as big fish chase little fish. Pulses and globs of iridescence energize, glow, and fade in our quarter wave. Beneath the surface, heat-lightning flickers betray deeper beings. Almost on cue, accompanied by my mental calliope music, dolphins appear, green-white etchings on the black plate of the sea. Their loops and rolls seem to form a cosmic time exposure. Icelight splashes and underwater illumination let us follow the porpoises below the surface. The individual performers are homogenized into choreography that gives me the joyously naughty sense of catching Nature in the act.

Chapter Fifteen

Die Meilesteine zur Freiheit—the milestones to freedom. In KZ Lager Dachau the sign was painted in huge letters on the roof of the *Haft*, the detention building, as though it were some sort of billboard for the damned. The milestones to freedom were *Arbeitsamkeit, Sauberkeit, und Ehrlichkeit*—willingness to work, cleanliness, and honesty. And the main gate to the camp bore the now-famous inscription *Arbeit macht frei*—Work makes you free.

Dachau was the nerve center of the concentration camp system. It was the first concentration camp that the Nazis opened after taking power. Its first commandant was Heinrich Himmler. It was near the geographical center, too, of the Reich. As the Allies and Russians squeezed the Germans tighter, more and more prisoners were shipped back to Dachau. The milestones we passed on our five-day cattle-car journey there from Schirmeck seemed good ones—Ragnvald and I were in a car with all Norwegians, including Tore, Ole, and Erik. We'd found

Erik on the siding in Schirmeck. He had "our" tin of meat. He wanted to trade it for bread, but a French prisoner came at him with a rock and tried to kill him for it, so he stopped trying to bargain. Still, because of the way the cars were loaded, we got an extra tin. Split between forty men, it made no great difference, but it was something extra, something on the good side.

We could see out of the cattle car only when someone opened the locked door from the outside. Our little ship rolling across Germany, . . . through the Schwartzwald . . . across the Atlantic . . . out to Bora Bora . . . plenty of fantasy time and, relatively speaking, no real problems. The transport to Dachau was an island of calm.

We had bread and meat. There was room to lie down half the time. Our only disagreements came about the war. Over half of us, myself included, said that it would be over in fourteen days or less. The Allies were pounding southern Germany day and night. If the guns we'd heard at Natzweiler were artillery, even tanks, wouldn't they be rolling along behind us, faster even than this stop-and-go train? There were no troops around here, we theorized. Strike through the south and then on to Berlin! It would be nice to be back in Grini to get the war news. Back in my family's flat, for that matter. Sylvei wouldn't let me listen, she'd be telling me the real story before I heard it on the radio. Kirsten wouldn't listen herself. She might be old enough now, though. What kind of innocence would the Nazis take from her, and when?

When we got to Dachau, capos were sent into the barracks yard as individual prisoners. In an alleyway between two barracks they ambushed Bull. Just five prisoners to begin with, but by the time they'd shouted his name—"The Bull, Bull goes, Bull Falls!"—there were twenty-five at least who wanted a piece of demolishing him. I hated him, too. I was on the fringe. I never got to him. He grunted, threw his weight around, and tossed and bruised a number of scarecrows before their weight got him to the ground. A Belgian prisoner, himself a bully who shook other prisoners down for extra food, stomped twice with his clog on Bull's Adam's apple. Wheezing, whistling gasps came from the big man, but not a word of surrender. The Belgian was taking too long. Others gouged and squeezed at Bull's ruptured throat. Then guards broke it up, but Bull was now just another body to burn.

The prisoner who hanged until the guard dug a hole for his feet, the guilty Russian who stole the meat tin, the despicable Bull . . . all three died in front of my eyes. If there was any crossbow sound of souls exiting, I didn't hear it. Three deaths, three different fables to explain them, but they left fatally similar corpses. Guilt, innocence, terror, revenge . . . whatever words we used, the bodies looked all the same.

There were prisoners from all over Europe in Dachau. It was big, five to ten times as big as Natzweiler. We didn't mind missing out on the "personal touch," because the SD in Dachau didn't consider NN prisoners to be a special category. They seemed not even to know what NN meant. As a consequence, we were assigned barracks in the regular camp. They even washed us. Suddenly we were no longer already dead.

Maybe it was Bull's ghost getting revenge, or probably just the luck of the draw, but we soon had to leave. Whether they finally discovered what NN meant or we just made a convenient "shipment," we were put back in cattle cars (once again, thankfully, our Cell 27 group stayed together) and sent away.

Ottobrun, near Munich, was small (only about a thousand prisoners) and rural. And there wasn't much work to do. I had the best job. There was a heap of carrots—a mountain, really, twenty-five feet square. I got to sort them. Most of them were rotten, but there was more food in that mountain than I could imagine. No one stopped me from eating the rotten ones. In fact, no one stopped me from eating the few good ones.

The people of Ottobrun were not like the vacant-eyed mountain people near Natzweiler or the housewives of Dautmergen who spat at us and called us *Dreck* when we were marched through the streets. The people of Ottobrun were farmers. They'd often leave half a loaf of bread where prisoners working along a fence would find it. One prisoner came back from the fields with well-worn boots to replace his wooden clogs. Even more than material help, the people of Ottobrun gave us some human contact, some warmth of the kind we'd been missing, sorely missing, for a long, long time.

Still, Ole became progressively withdrawn. In Ottobrun there were lots of chances to scavenge. Norwegians shared what they could, and he was offered things, once or twice something almost irresistible like an apple not badly bruised or a bite of luscious-looking *Wienerschnitzel* that Erik had gotten from a farm girl on her way to town, and he refused. He refused every bite of every treat. Food like that could mean staying alive. That's what worried us. Ole seemed just to have run down. He ate the normal meals, he seemed to relish them, but it was clear that he wouldn't walk across the room to eat more. It made no sense.

One afternoon I was sitting along a fence near a line of pear trees with Ole and Erik and our guard. It was a low fence, and the closest pear tree had two pears unpicked, high in its spindly upper branches. We had some vague thoughts of waiting for the guard to start toward the other side of the compound and then boosting one of us over the fence to go after the pears. That is, Erik and I were scheming. We figured we might use Ole as a stepladder to get over the wire.

Down our valley, about fifty feet above the pear trees, came two screaming twin-engined airplanes. Until I picked myself off the ground and thought for a second, I didn't realize they were British Mosquitoes. The same tearing whine, the same whooshing pass a second time—then another pair, damn near wingtip to wingtip, powering down the valley. We heard bomb blasts, and then a third pair were approaching. I had read and fantasized about these flyweight plywood bombers, thought that

I'd heard them over Oslo, over Natzweiler, even Dachau, but here they were—real ones! We lay in the grass and watched them climb and dive and stack and strafe.

"They don't seem too worried about the Luftwaffe," Erik said.

"I could see their faces, the pilots' faces. One guy had a mustache, a handlebar, I swear," I said.

Before long they started their exit, back out the valley, pair by pair passing over us. I wanted to jump up and wave, but a person on the ground is a target, whether he's from Bavaria or Norway. When they'd wheeled back into the west, dots about to disappear over the horizon down the center of the valley floor, we noticed Ole. Curled up and silent, he obviously felt none of the excitement, grasped none of the significance of low-level bombing this deep into Germany. It was hard, even, to get him to help us bring down the two pears. Had he broken? Was he just letting the waves of crap break over him? Maybe he knew something that I didn't.

There were sixty-one Norwegians in Ottobrun. After the raid we all talked about home. It won't be long! We'll be there soon! The Krauts can't hold out. The Brits are coming . . . just as in Africa and Italy.

It was September of 1944. Along the Isar and in the other small valleys cutting south into the Bavarian Alps there were still no signs of autumn. Nevertheless it proved long winter.

Chapter Sixteen

The sun must be up. It says so in our tables. It's nearly o600, so there is sun, but we can't see much of it. Spitting rain, low cloud, and chunks of mist make it seem like midnight. Tone is at the helm. Chris and I nestle below. He's got another three hours until he has to go up and get wet. I just came off duty. I'm out of my wet-weather gear now. I lay it out next to the companionway, to dry, to jump into. The breeze is southeast, Force Five (right around twenty knots). *Tresbelle* is leaving a nice straight wake, but the seas are rolling her and slapping at her from abeam. At the beginning of this trip Chris and I worried when we lost the steerer. Tone had never steered much offshore. She's picked it up. She stands her watches well. She's intelligent, she listens, she's not afraid to ask about things. Two weeks ago I wouldn't be relaxing below leaving her up there in foggy Force Five and devilish steering. Now I'm just raring to get in my quarterberth and hibernate.

"Bels? Bels?"

Even in Tone's sexy rasp the words aren't welcome. Without moving much in my quilt I manage a "Coming, dear." I can almost hear the creaks as I regretfully roll my old bones out of the berth. Before I look for my seaboots in the pile of wet gear at the foot of the steps I stick my head out.

"Sorry," Tone says, "but I can't hold zero six eight or anything like it. We need some trim, and maybe the jib should come off."

"Be right there."

I throw on trousers and a chamois shirt, the boots—no socks—and the top to my foul-weather gear. A fireman has to hit the pole and go whether it's a brushfire or four alarms. It can be a fireman's jump, thirty seconds or less, to get on deck if we have to, but it's smarter and safer in the long run to take more time if you've got it. If I ran out there in my skivvies, I'd be too cold and too ridiculous to be much help after a minute or two. And if all of us spent our off-watch time putting out fires or the deck watch, we'd be too worn out and pissed off to function at all. I can tell that it's no emergency, but out of habitual concern I decide not to take the time to put on my foul-weather bottoms.

"I'm getting headed all of the time—the breeze is one forty now. It was one sixty. So we need some trim to the sails. And there is thunder over there." She gestures over her left shoulder toward a spot astern of us.

Tone looks every inch the seafarer. I wonder if Ellen will take like this to the sea. But then it was a wise sailor who said, "Don't look for a wife who loves to sail into the gale—what excuse then will *you* have to turn back?"

I listen for the thunder. Beneath the creak of the mainsheet blocks, the slap and slosh of the seas, *Tresbelle's* many sounds,

I hear dull rumbles. The mist spits thicker; I wish I'd put on those trousers.

"Throw in a reef, for safety's sake?"

"Go to it, Leif," says Tone, "but I can't hold zero six eight unless we trim some."

"Just do what you can till we get the reef in." I loosen the main halyard and smile. Chris has come on deck. One of the joys this trip has been having an extra hand, and Chris has always been it. I can't remember him sleeping through a sail change.

"As we always say, *Tresbelle's* a happy ship, and I'm just no happy when I'm in my bunk." He smiles with all the pomposity of one doing the work of three.

We tie in the reef.

"I'm still getting headed. We've got to trim close-hauled," Tone says. We trim, thunder lumbers closer.

"Yeah, it's backing right around from south to north," Chris says. The rain spatters now instead of spitting.

"Might make sense to tack before the squall."

"Good."

"Ready about?"

"Ready."

"Ready here."

"Hard alee."

The jib sheet snakes up and off the leeward winch drum, slaps in-out-in on the shrouds, slams forward of the mast, catches on the forestay, then slithers home to my side, where I winch it in. The mainsail tends itself. We're sailing now on a new course ninety degrees from the old.

The rain hisses down on the waves. The breeze lightens. We feel the chill. "Must be an iceberg regatta out there," Chris says.

Tone holds her left hand out and slightly behind her. "I don't know about bergs, but the squall is over there."

"What do you think about the headsail?" I ask Chris.

"We don't want to have to douse it in the squall. I think ou're right."

Chris loosens the halyard, and passes if aft to Tone, and we ;o forward.

"Come off the wind till we blanket it! Keep coming. That's ;ood. Steady there," I call aft.

"All set."

She lowers the sail. "Keep coming . . . faster . . . hold it . . come on . . . wait . . . all the way," Chris directs. He .nd I smother the billowing jib as it drops. We lash it down .nd flee aft.

More rain, less wind. We're standing upright now, going ery slow.

The growls in the distance grow to impressive kkkkkkkiiick..booooms". The chill deepens, the rain contin-.es. I'm glad all three of us are on deck.

"Two hands for yourself in a knockdown. *Tresbelle* can take :are of herself. Just hang on, stay aboard." A thunderclap .unctuates my oration to the crew. Like a crisp slap from the .ack of Aeolus's hand, the first puff hits. Our boat shudders, .ips well down to leeward, buries her rail momentarily, then .oams ahead. I ease the main, Tone spins and wrestles at the .heel until we settle straight, and *Tresbelle* lunges ahead. The .ain slants sideways. It's tough to see, impossible to hear. It .tings. Suddenly it's blowing at least fifty. *Tresbelle* races up to .ull speed with only her tiny reefed mainsail flying. Perched, .lert, but with nothing really to do, we flank Tone as she steers .hrough the squall.

"*Close reach and follow the wind around. Okay?*"

"*No . . . what?*"

"*Forget the course . . . sail the wind.*"

"*Gotcha.*"

The breeze backs, lightens, then veers hard. We're now on . course back to Boston. I'm afraid to tack.

"Hang on!" Chris says, and we screech the wrong way for

painful minutes until we're let around pointing closer and closer
again toward Arran Isle. Behind the squall is crisp, puffy air
from the northwest and the sun.

"If I might be so bold as the skipper of this vessel . . . where
the hell are we?" I ask Chris as we peel down for bed.

"On the back side of a cold front, sliding down a nor'wester."

"Thanks, Magellan. What I was asking about was the mile-
age remaining between us and the haggis. Where exactly would
you draw your little X on our chart of this vast sea?"

"Uh-huh! Well, if that's the way you want to be. You know
we haven't had any sun sights in four days. Might not be bad
at noon, but it looks like it's already clouding over some. So
running down the dead reckoning from that position from the
Canadians . . . about five hundred and ten miles to go and
we're something like here, in very round figures."

"Well, the coast of Ireland is not smooth enough for round
figures, but that's great. Five hundred miles to go!"

"Five hundred and ten."

"Three days! I'll be talking to Ellen in three days!"

"Or six, or nine, or thirteen."

"Three days!"

Chris works some more on the charts, I write in the log.
Then I resume the letter to Ellen to tell her the good news—
three days. Then I try a page or two of war story. The storm
was brief. I didn't do much, but it's left me with amazing
energy.

I try to use Ellen as my model audience. What would she
need to know? Care to know about prewar Norway? That's a
start. And I scratch out three pages before turning in.

Chris is ready to go on deck. He sees me with half an eye
open and stops to brief me on what's happening upstairs.

"Pointed precisely for Arran Island at seven point eight knots."

"Three days and counting . . . one, two, three."

"Come on, Bels. You know anything can happen."

"We've weathered the storm. *Tresbelle* came shining through. Anything could happen, but we could fly over five hundred miles in three days. Have you got a moment before you go on deck?"

"Sure."

"It's the damn book. I wrote some last night—I mean, this morning—before I went to bed, and when I read it over it sounded awful. Dry and stiff. But I don't know how else to talk about things that seem so important."

"That's natural, Bels. It's tough material, it's old, it's forbidding . . . you haven't been able to tackle it for forty years. The first time through all of that is bound to show. A story like yours would make real authors struggle. What do you expect from a beginner like you? I mean it. It's natural. Nobody starts writing the way they finish up. You'll loosen up, you'll get hot. But you've got to do it. . . . Of course you don't have to do it. You don't have to write it, but if you want to write it . . . you've got to write it. How's that?"

Wrapped in eiderdown, I wasn't quite sure which way was up. Out of the thumping and banging of *Tresbelle* doing seven and a half knots across lumpy seas came an upheaval and a monster crash. I jerked clear of the covers. I was looking into deep green water. "Jesus!"

Through the port I saw nothing but ocean. I was looking up from my back in the berth, through the port over my head. Swirling, foamy seawater. "I'm underwater? We're underwater? Good God!" Struggling uphill and out from the lowest point in the boat, I was confused and scared. As I elbowed and clawed my way out of the bunk to the foot of the tilted companionway ladder, I began to feel the boat coming back onto an evener keel. I figured out that we'd broached and filled the

cockpit. A broach is the beginning of a capsize. Boats like
Tresbelle have weighted keels big enough to keep them from
turning over, but this time we had been damn near there.

Who was on deck? Were they still there?

The companionway was partly closed, but, peeking over the
top board, I saw Chris crotch-deep in the cockpit. Beside him
were weird marine-looking objects. Dolphins? Killer whales?
No, just the black buckets from aft come adrift and floating.

"Just lost her, Bels," Chris shouted. "Everything's okay, I
think. Just didn't stop her in time and she wiped right up and
broached."

"How are you?"

'Pissed off. Embarrassed."

"Gus told me they had watches where they broached every
fifteen minutes on the TwoStar."

"Well, Gus wasn't sailing in a silly twenty-five-knot wind
with reefs in."

"What's this, the roller coaster?" Tone shouted from beside
me in the doorway.

Cockpits never drain fast enough, but ours was emptied in
less than a minute. I was on deck soon after in my undies.
Chris was fine. We just needed to get the jib down. The wind
had come ahead again, and it was iffy carrying it on a spinnaker pole. I hate to work on deck in bare feet, so, in boots and
skivvies, I doused the jib and dropped the pole. Then I felt
sick.

"Shall we heave to?"

"We need the rest."

Heaving to is like tying the boat to a tree. The motion is
much better when you ride with the boat's bow to the seas.
We weren't getting any closer to Ireland by heaving to, but we
weren't beating ourselves up either. Chris was happy to turn
in. Tone was in her bunk, I had just snuggled into mine. This
was a good move, resting now to sail hard later.

The engine started.

By itself our diesel kicked over. "What the hell?"

In my new pair of dry undies I bolted on deck again, throttled it down, and turned it off. I'd never seen or heard of spontaneous ignition. The damn thing had just fired up on its own. We were all in our bunks. Good Lord. Maybe the engine was a genie. If I said "Engine," would it start again?

"Engine."

Whew. There was no doubt; that wave we had taken aboard had screwed up our electrics. But what to do?

Chris and I took all things electric off the engine, dried them, examined them, and put them back. It was hard to dry anything out l ere, but we thought we had it. I hooked the positive pole on the battery. I was tightening the ground when I heard and smelled the sizzle.

"The pole's melting!" said Chris.

He was right. The positive pole was gurgling and smoking. We ripped the system apart and left it apart.

Chapter Seventeen

For what seems like hours our train has been stopping and starting. Through the slats you can tell that it's dark. When we were going faster, the rain came through. Now it just drums on the roof. We've been inside this dark box . . . three days? Four? Maybe five? I think four. Some time ago the shit bucket overflowed. There are only thirty of us. We can move around . . . we shit now in the far corner.

We've saved some bread, but if we don't stop soon we'll have nothing. Stopping and starting some more. We stop. Lurch ahead, stop again. I hear voices. A town? A camp? The voices aren't German. Good God, have they sent us to Czechoslovakia? Hungary? We can hear them working to open the car in front. That's Polish . . . they're speaking Polish. My God. Where the hell are we?

The door opens. There are two men, SS. They motion us down, and they order us in some language . . . it's not German. Polish SS! Their storm coats shine in the driving rain.

"*Norweger*," one of them says. The other orders us out "*Raus! Rausschmeissen! Schnell!*" The Polish SS speak German that is accented strangely. By now we've figured out what *Raus* and *los* mean, though.

Capos, Polish capos. No one from our Cell 27 group speaks Polish. I hope they all speak German.

There's a gravel area on the siding where we stand. Around it are ruts and puddles. Wherever this is, it must have been raining for days. The capos don't waste any time. They roust us, with bare hands and clubs, off the gravel and through the mud. It's fifteen minutes of marching to the camp; most of us lose our clogs in the mud on the way.

It's September, and it's cold in the rain. Dautmergen is the name of the camp. Is this Poland? Are they throwing us to the Russians? Could you tell if this is Poland in the rain and dark? At least it's not in the mountains like Natzweiler. "*Los! Los!*" We stop in the mud. There's a field off to our right. Some tents, a shack or two. This is it? This is nothing. It's not even a camp. No barracks. Nothing. I see the tents, but I see people sleeping outside of them in the rain. Oh shit. This is beginning to make the cattle car look cozy.

The "road" we're on oozes across the hillside to a fence, where we stop. Tents off to our right are cluttered together on a low hill. There are gullies and ravines where the runoff water cuts the road. Where we are there's a small stream across our feet. The capos can't find a place for us. The SS go into their tent. Ragnvald and I look for shelter, any kind of shelter. Ole is with us. Erik's talking to one of the capos. Such confusion is not what we're used to. They have nowhere to put us. They don't much care. Erik says two trains arrived yesterday. The capos make pillow motions with their hands. Sweet dreams. They too disappear inside tents.

"Thanks, you pricks. Don't choke on your kielbasa."

We're sleeping in the mud. We're wet, chilled, and we're sleeping in the mud in the rain. Any colder and some of us won't wake up. Head-scratching, shuffling. Finally Ragnvald says, "If the bastards are going to treat us like dogs, we might as well act like them. Dogs in the mountains." It's a shitty idea, but it's the best one we have. Like Rantas, Mette, General Wavell, and Ruge, we burrow into the mud, huddle together, and get a wink or two of sleep while we keep each other warm.

Coffee call came at four-thirty. After coffee call they set us right to work. At last at Dautmergen the work is not as nonsensical as the quarrying at Natzweiler. We are building barracks. Shoveling trenches, carrying stones and planks. The barracks are for us, so we work hard, but the tough work is made tougher by our calorie intake . . . eight hundred and lower a day. The SD has plans for a big camp here, for strip mining. Before long we will be digging up the loam or whatever it is that they get oil, shale oil, from.

The Allied raids were more and more successful. Damage was everywhere. We heard rumors the Allies had crossed the Rhine. And the Nazis were building this big new *Konzentrationslager* here in Dautmergen. They just wouldn't give up. Maybe they had some monster weapon that would save them. God, that would be horrible. How many people were dying every day in this stupid war? Couldn't they just stop it? Wouldn't that be a good place to start making up for what they'd done? Think of the lives that would save! Who were these Nazis, anyway? Would Hitler destroy everyone, everything? They had no hope to win. Why did they keep on.

We built new barracks, and prisoners kept coming, so they had us convert the horse barns. By then we had been in the camp long enough to get out of the tents and move inside a barn. There was a very colorful old poster on the wall. It showed a handsome horse's head and read something like: "Do not fail to supply clean water, good food, ventilation, comfortable shelter, and conscientious care."

"For the horses!" Erik said. "How to treat the horses, in the barns! I'll take that. Give me that kind of care. I'm a horse. Tell them I'm a goddam horse."

Every day we go into the fields. Every day fewer of us come back. Exhaustion, yes, but they are making room for "new blood," they are "pruning" the work force. Most of the capos seem to have quotas with the SS. They have their work assignments, but part of the sport for them is weeding out their crews. And then there are those SS who order prisoners to throw their caps in a field. "Now go and get them." When you do you're shot for "escaping." When you refuse you're shot for refusing. Capos sometimes single out one prisoner and try to work him to death. The prisoners are most often tough enough to survive the work, so as a reward for survival they're usually made to kneel beside a ditch on the way home and shot. Most times the capos don't go to the trouble of transporting the corpses back to camp. There are details every couple of days to retrieve the bodies from the ditches and fields around Dautmergen and deliver them to our growing morgue.

Even though I cheat and cut as many corners as I can, the work is very hard. I am tall, and when we carry beams I get more of the weight. The conditions don't help. Shelter is still the minimum. The latrine is a slippery pole. Sit on it, perch over the pit, hold your breath against the stench, put your feet in the mud . . . it's terrible. The gong is beaten at four in the morning and we work sixteen hours a day. And every day it seems to get colder. Our uniforms are not thick enough to keep the wind off. No clothes, no heat, nothing but each other to keep warm with. We are nothing but bone, which gives new meaning to the term "bone-chilling."

One day Ole came back from the field. He spoke to us. He was washed out and listless much of the time, but he could still talk! He was bigger than the rest of us, so they had taken him to work with a framing crew. Most of them were Polish. Ole told us what the Polish workers told him:

"Franciszek told me what happened in Warsaw. At the end of the summer, not very long ago. The Red Army pushed the Germans right back to Warsaw. Inside the city, Franciszek told me, they were ready to fight, to set Warsaw free. The Polish fighters heard a broadcast from the Red Army. The radio said to rise up. Together we will set Warsaw free, the broadcast said. The people in Warsaw wanted to set themselves free. The Germans had all of the firepower, though. Still, they could almost see the Russian army, so they rose up. Inside the streets of Warsaw they began to fight the Germans. They rose up, and right then the Russians just stopped. They sat on the other side of the river, the Vilna. They didn't cross. They didn't help at all.

"Franciszek said at the beginning they were winning. Some of his friends captured a tank. They were doing fine fighting the Germans with the tank, using it for cover. Then they broke the treads on it. The Nazis blew it up.

"My friend laughed about one story. There was a Gestapo man caught in a hotel room with a girl when the fighting started. They caught him. There was a trial—counsel for the defense, prosecution, three judges, a real trial. They sentenced him to die and killed him in the courtyard of the hotel. The next day the girl came back and showed the Germans where their bunkers were. The Nazis used grenades to drive them out and then shot everyone.

"Stukas bombed the streets with fire bombs. The Germans just wanted to destroy everything. The Russians wouldn't even send fighters up or fire at the Stukas with their guns. They were in easy range. Franciszek said that near the end of the first ten days he looked up to see Halifaxes, British Halifaxes. The sky was purple and he could see the supplies tumbling out. Most of them went to the Germans, though. Americans dropped supply containers. He could see thousands falling, it seemed. They counted two hundred and eighty-eight for all of the underground the next day. The Russians were across the river. The British and Americans flew from Italy and France. Franciszek says the Russians were trying to kill off all of the Poles who aren't Communist. They just about made it, he says. The whole city was rubble when the Nazis caught him. One of every four people in Warsaw was killed or wounded. Christ, can you imagine that? And the Russian army just stayed on the other side of the Vilna and watched."

We asked Ole to tell us more, but he said nothing. Imagine, fighting to the end of that battle in Warsaw and then being shipped off to Dautmergen to live in the mud or be shot by an SS guard.

Since we'd arrived I'd had violent dysentery. Dehydration (we had only a cupful of water a day), cramps, fever. It didn't get any better. And there was the matter of my trousers. The capos wouldn't give us a break when we had to shit. They wouldn't let us pull our pants down, so we shit in them. Five, ten, fifteen times a day. We couldn't wash them, so we lived in them. I was burned raw. I got so even I couldn't stand my own smell. I was not alone, but I was miserable. Finally I got into the tent they called a hospital. It was a great way to lengthen your chances of coming back from work by not going out at all.

Jahren, one of our original group from Cell 27 at Grini, was in there, too. I knew that he had been arrested for commando work in the mountains in Norway. He told me more as we lay in the tent, and after the war I figured out that he had been one of the supporting players for the famous "heavy water" raid. In 1938 an experiment under the direction of German physicist Otto Hahn led to the discovery of nuclear fission. Albert Einstein wrote to President Roosevelt outlining the possibility that the discovery could lead to a superweapon. The Germans already had the lead. In 1942, Winston Churchill and Roosevelt met in Washington. They agreed to pool

knowledge and resources to press ahead with their own efforts
to develop the bomb, and they also underlined the need to do
whatever possible to offset the Nazi lead. This led to a focus
on the Norsk Hydro plant at Rjukan, Norway, the sole known
source of heavy water for the Nazi atomic efforts.

The first attempt to knock out the plant was an elaborate
commando raid. Two thirty-four-man teams, each in its own
glider, were towed the unprecedented distance of four hundred
miles from England. Weather, logistics, and mechanical fail-
ures all contributed to the disaster. Both gliders crash-landed.
The survivors from the first were shot immediately despite the
fact that they were in uniform. The five surviving commandos
from the second team were questioned first and then later shot.

The Norwegian commandos who were to prepare the landing sites for the first operation were still in place on the Har-
danger plateau, near Lake Tinnsjö. Six expert ski troops from
the Royal Norwegian Army volunteers in England parachuted
in to join them. The plant was nearly inaccessible and heavily
guarded, and many approaches to it were mined. The group
climbed a six-hundred-foot rock cliff to gain access, planted
charges without opposition, and set off explosions that destroyed
both the stockpiled heavy water and the equipment needed to
make more. Then they scattered.

One commando wound up eating dinner in the same hotel
dining room as General Redeiss and Gauleiter Terboven, who
came to supervise the manhunt. Jahren was in the Mil-Org in
the area, and I believe that he either transported or sheltered
two of the group. At any rate, he was arrested and joined us at
Grini. I didn't know anything about the raid then, but I knew
Jahren was in bad shape. Imagine if the Nazis got their superweapon. Maybe they could still win the war. Maybe without
Jahren and that raid they would have done it.

We had never been close friends, but he had no one else. I
didn't know what to do. Sometimes I could get him to laugh,
and I thought I could see life in his eyes. I told him stories and

jokes. He laughed, very weakly. He had tuberculosis, galloping tuberculosis. It was like a beast, a monster gobbling at him, sucking and slobbering and smothering his life. It was strange; after a while he just got so sick there was nothing to do. I could see him struggling. I tried to help. It was like trying to stop a house from burning when it's already engulfed. There was nothing his spirit or his mind could do.

Finally, he turned to me and said, "I've had it. I'm going to die."

I wanted to save him, I wanted to do something or say something.

"Say hello to my parents," he said, and he died.

He was the first of our group to die. I had thought talking to him would help. I had thought I could keep him alive.

Jahren's death seemed like a signal that I had to get out of Dautmergen. It seemed suicide to stay on there. Right after he died, someone gave me some opium and carbon tablets. I had a pleasant reverie and, what's more, my dysentery improved. But I was not very anxious to be released. And so I spent a few nights in our new hospital barracks. Patients died every night. Every morning an SS man came through and pulled the gold teeth from the corpses. That sound is hard to forget. Pulling the teeth took a real effort with dentist's pliers. It made a crunch, a crack that agonized almost into a squeal before the final *plop* of release. Sometimes the SS man would be in a hurry and just break the teeth. As I lay in bed on hospital mornings it occasionally seemed almost comical, but usually my stomach heaved when I heard those sounds.

The Norwegians in general stuck together. I still had no desire to work in the cold, but they kicked me out of the hospital when my dysentery improved. Between the morning meal and going to work there was occasionally some time outside. It was cold. We'd put our backs together for warmth and sing. It was my form of prayer. Back to back with my prisoner brothers, singing the Bergen songs in a slow Bergen accent, I'd sing,

"They're not going to get us." It helped. Norwegians have been going off to sea since the long ships; we stick together. "We all live in the same village." And together we sang, "They're not going to get us!"

I hadn't seen Ragnvald in quite some time. We went outside the gate, into the fields. I slipped away to see if I could find him. Just outside the gate was the tent where they stacked bodies awaiting burial. The stench inside was worse than in the *Scheisserei*—the shittery. This was because most of the dead had died of dysentery. People in the last stages of dysentery literally "shit their rectums." Surrounding me were stacks of corpses, many of which had exploded rectums hanging by a few feet of intestine, rectums that seeped and dripped. I expected it, I was used to it, but the sight joined the smell to make me gag and start to puke. Next to these stinking, dangling, grinning bodies sat Ragnvald. Knees drawn up around his ears like a kangaroo, he was leaning up against the lee side of the corpse pile. He was startled until he recognized me. Then he said, earnestly, urgently, "shhh. Shhh. Don't tell anyone. You won't tell anyone? It's my secret. It's my place."

He sounded crazy. He sounded as though this stinking tent full of grossly deformed stiffs were his golden bower, his castle. What a lovely secret. I realized, though, that Ragnvald had hit upon something. He could conserve his energy in relative warmth. One way to make sure you didn't get shot during work detail was not to go on work detail. But he sounded so desperate, so querulous, so strange. He sounded nothing at all like the man who had run up the mountain with me at Natzweiler, who had marched all of these miles with me on a leg that didn't really even work, who had never let any guard or capo intimidate him. I could understand that this grisly place might get to his brain. Should I break him free of this? Drag him back to camp for his own good? Then, in the shit-stink and gloom of this God-cursed meathouse, Ragnvald winked at me.

Ragnvald continued to be counted in and out with his work group while hiding away the workday with his unbending friends. However, they did away with the tent two weeks later to make way for a mass grave.

I was running out of time. I could tell. Murder, disease, starvation, exhaustion—they were getting too close. I had to get out if I was going to live. There were rumors of a "sick transport" to take prisoners too ill to work back to Dachau. That was another of the brilliantly unsolvable choices the Gestapo delighted in throwing our way. The odds of survival through the winter were abyssmal. With stepped-up work details, with capos given wider liberty to kill, with the current chaos deepening as the Polish SS let things slide, and with the joys of strip mining ahead, I saw little hope. On the other hand, sick transports more often than not just shuttled the sickly to a nearby gravesite where they were done away with. Yet I needed to get out, and the sick transport was the only way. It was a chance I had to take.

I did everything I could to get my name on the sick-transport list. My recurring dysentery made me eligible. And one or two of the Polish doctors were okay. But I hated our "hospital". It was almost as sickening as the morgue. The doctors and SS still robbed the dead of their teeth, and the sights and sounds of death, never far away, still jolted me. But the hospital barracks had also become the center for the pretty boys in camp, the young, smooth-cheeked Polish boys who kept themselves alive (and well-fed) by "servicing" *die Prominenten*—the prisoner ruling class of "Aryan" Poles. The romantic tangles that grew up around these preening kids bred demeaning jealousies, even murder.

My way of "courting" the two Polish doctors I had come to know was not sexual. I was just around, eager, and helpful enough to earn their good favor. Finally I got the news—I was on the list for the sick transport.

It was a chill October morning. They marched the sick

transport out to buses, buses headed for the train at Schönberg. There were two buses. One went toward Schönberg. The
other, mine, took off in the opposite direction.

I guess this is it, I thought Maybe they'll just gun us down
in a field and be done with it.

My brain was numb. I weighed ninety pounds. I guess I
really belonged on the sick transport. I couldn't get too excited
about dying. It was just another in the series of things you had
to put up with. I wondered if Ragnvald would ever find out
what had happened to me.

We turned a corner. The bus wound into a little road that
snaked around until finally, coming from the opposite side of
the tracks, it reached the station. I couldn't believe it. We had
come to Schönberg another way . . . that was all. The other
bus was there. I guess when you've been already dead, there's
nothing special about more of the same.

On the platform I saw Juliusen. He was the only other Norwegian on the sick transport. When I got off the bus I went to
him. We had met in Natzweiler. He was maybe ten years
older, a stoker in the merchant marine. He was also a part of
one of the most heroic and most disastrous Norwegian efforts
of the war. A bunch of sailors, most of them able-bodied rather
than officers, took it upon themselves to liberate the ten Norwegian merchant ships (lighters, whalers, trawlers, and a
freighter or two) interned in Göteborg, Sweden, at the out-
break of the war. They wanted to commandeer them and sail
them to England. Juliusen went along, escaping from Norway, joining the ship, taking over, getting her out of intern-
ment and onto the high seas. But then they ran into problems.
His was one of the four ships sunk by U-boats. He was picked
up. For his heroism at sea they made him an NN prisoner.
He, too, was on the sick transport back to Dachau.

Chapter Eighteen

Juliusen and I waited beside the tracks. It was important to get a good spot. There were more than a hundred people waiting for each car. If you are trampled for a whole trip, if you have to fight the people around you, your chances of getting out of the car alive are not good. We were only two. We needed a corner. Juliusen was thin, like the rest of us. He still had a stoker's arms. His biceps, like mine, were just a string of what they had been, but his wrists were knotty. Massive gristle and sinew that didn't fit the time or place, those wrists were what I will always remember about Juliusen.

The train came. We gauged our spot, then we leaped. We were lucky as well as a bit quicker and stronger. We got our corner—something at our back, something to lean on. We never left the corner.

People kept jamming aboard. Between eighty and a hundred made it. The rest either went back to Dautmergen or to some

ditch on the way. When the doors closed, many of us sighed
and celebrated. "We made it!" Concentration camp prisoners
are hardly a healthy group, and we were the sickest and the
sorriest of the prisoners. I wondered if any of us would make
it. Transports before had been all Norwegians to a car and no
more than thirty. Maybe as many as ninety were in this car, a
madhouse mix from madhouse Dautmergen, and it was bound
to be a feverish fight for survival. I wondered if we would make
it. Hell on wheels crammed with coughing, delirious pilgrims.
We set off.

We had half a loaf of bread each. No water, no space, hardly
any air, just half a precious loaf. Juliusen and I still were happy
to be underway. He told me how he'd hated Dautmergen—
"the mud, the work, the queers, no one understood you, Jesus!"
I tried to tell him about Dachau, about the old cellblocks and
the cypress trees, about the hospital—it was supposed to be the
best of the camps. About the "milestones." He told me some
things about his time at sea. I told him about my sailing, but
before long we found we just had to grin and bear it. It was
too miserable to talk, even to think. We just held on. If we'd
had to wrestle and push for a spot for the whole trip . . .

The days rolled by. I'm not sure whether it was three or four
or six or fourteen. I slept and sweated and shit in my pants. I
fought to hold our corner, I nibbled a little bread. I had day
dreams and night dreams. I rocked in time with the car and
tried to keep my mind from sliding into jelly. Happy pilgrims!
An overflowing shit bucket, and a carful of death and disease,
yo ho ho!

Bodies lay all around. They were strewn in all positions.
Living on dead, dead on living, it looked like a battlefield where
two wierd, shrunken tribes massacred one another. The Beast
came in. I wasn't certain how. Sniffing the air, grinning, it
pawed around. It had broken teeth covered with spit and blood.
You could see the little tufts of hair under its lip when it grinned.
It licked its caked lips and started to pick through the bodies.
The Beast poked and turned over bodies, rummaging through

the pile, moving and slurping from one end of the car to the other. It lifted and pried and then . . . *wham*. Juliusen grabbed the Beast by the wrist.

The Beast glared with yellow eyes. Juliusen held tight. The Beast gave a snuffling growl. Juliusen held fast. The Beast squealed and jerked away. Juliusen held firm.

"I know something that doesn't die."

Twisting and raging, the Beast squealed, thrashed, pulled free at last. There was a crack—like pulling teeth. The Beast was free, but in his grip Juliusen still held a sinewed arm tufted with hair and dripping lifeblood. The Beast never came back.

The train rocked ahead. You couldn't keep track of the days. People had been dying all along. Their stares never looked away. I didn't know how to hold on to myself. I felt my mind fluttering, twitching. Juliusen sang to me, "We're headed home, lad, homeward bound. Pull one time for your home."

When they opened our car in Dachau, it took Ian Hopper, whose job it was to record new arrivals, almost half an hour to find anyone alive. Some bodies had begun to decompose. They unloaded more than sixty corpses. There were only a dozen of us left alive. They put us, four or five to the barrow, on wagons and wheeled us to the infirmary. Because the infirmary at Dachau was much better than most and because of Ian, who worked there, too, Juliusen and I survived our transport to Dachau.

We were washed, changed and fed . . . hot porridge at that. "Breakfast," Ian called it. My grandmother was English, and I could speak the language pretty well, and so we understood each other. Ian took pleasure in talking, and I in listening . . . it meant I was alive. Often he'd address me as "old man." Each time he did, Juliusen, whose English was more limited, would smile and guffaw as though there were some monstrous joke. Finally I realized that even though I was still a teenager, in my current condition I looked enough like a sixty-year-old that Juliusen thought Ian was giving me the respect due an elder.

Chapter Nineteen

"I've had it! I've had it!"

Up the companionway comes Chris, a crazed, glazed look in his eye, foam at the corners of his mouth and a cooking pot on his head. "I've had it!" he shouts and bangs on the pot with a wooden spoon as he emerges from down below into the windless glare of our doldrums. He bangs on the pot with a wooden spoon and chants, "I've had it!"

Balmy? I ask myself. Has he really gone around the bend in three days of midocean calm?

He has, I see, a toothbrush in his teeth. It is not held like a toothbrush but clenched sideways, like a pirate's knife. It makes his constant I've-had-its sound fuzzy: "Owwwve additt."

It takes me a second to know what to make of him. I doubt my red-bearded bosun has really crossed the line, but he's not holding back in the charade at all.

"I've had it, too! I've had it!" I join in.

"You've had it?" Tone screeches from below. "You've had

it? What about me, goddammit? I've had it! I've had it up to
here!" From topside I can't tell where "here" is.

Chris marches forward, still banging his head with a spoon.
I don't know why, but I pick up the boat hook. I joust it up
and down in time to our chant. "We've had it. We've had it."

Tone sticks her head up. "Keep ranting . . . maybe you'll
stir up some wind. Three days! We should be in a Scottish
pub by now. Three days!"

Three days ago . . . let me see. First the breeze was light
from the east, then an hour or two of good southerly, but for
the last seventy-eight hours, we have gone nowhere. There has
been virtually nothing in the way of wind. Three weeks at sea
and only three days of calm. That's about average, but it's hard
to remember from time to time how frustrating and draining
the doldrums can be. Self-congratulation, too, is in order for
taking the northern route. Imagine what we'd have gotten if
we'd gone straight out into the flatlands between Land's End
and Boston. But we sure haven't closed much on Ireland
recently. When the wind dies, you sit back, say, "Give it an
hour," and try to relax. You could turn on the engine. I usually do, because everyone is always so focused on getting there,
but that's not always good. Running it for too long is almost
as irritating as the doldrums. The noise, vibrations, smell . . .
many sailboat engines lack elegance. We carry enough diesel
for only 260 or 270 miles, and we've used two thirds of that
generating for an hour a day. And now that we've got this
magic self-starting engine with its sizzling battery poles I've
been scared to try it at all until we really need it.

"I really have had it," says Chris in the last gasps of his
demonstration against the wind gods.

"I thought you were just being silly with the pot on your
head and everything, but then I saw the foam at the corners of
your mouth."

"I knew that would get you. I didn't want you to jump overboard, so I chomped on the toothbrush as a hint that the foam

was really toothpaste. I may be crazy, but I don't want to drive my old skipper up the mast."

"Oh, what tangled dental floss we weave . . . no, that's terrible, forget I said that. But I really *have* had it," offers Tone as she made her entrance from below.

"At least we're not slatting around so much anymore," I say.

"That *is* the worst."

"No, it was even worse in the beginning," Tone says, "When there were waves. No wind, and waves throwing us all over the place. I thought I was going to be seasick. I thought I was going to shoot you, Bels, or myself, or something."

"Water, water everywhere, and how the boards did shrink."

"What does that have to do with anything, Chris?"

"Tone, our trials are just chapters in the saga of human suffering." Chris grinned. "Like last night when you dumped the garbage over. Those cups. Wasn't that something. The way those two Styrofoam cups wound up upright. The way they just sat on the ocean as if it were a table. Nothing to skid them around, nothing to knock them over. I'll bet they're still standing like that in the middle of the Atlantic. But at least we can't see them anymore. Maybe they're ahead of us. Is there anything about Styrofoam cups in the sagas, Bels?"

I think the sagas probably have a lot to say about doldrums, but I don't want to hear any more. A sailor's relation with the wind gods is a sacred thing.

I leave them in the cockpit pondering my pronouncement while I rummage below for *Moxie*, Phil Weld's story of winning the OSTAR (Observer Singlehanded Transatlantic Race) in 1980. He was the first American ever to do it. Having all just taken arms against Aeolus, maybe we should listen to Phil. Phil was one of the century's best sailors, and wisest, too. He's dead now, but still, when Phil speaks, he is the E. F. Hutton of sailors.

Ever since I got becalmed in the Azores on the 1972 OSTAR, I've strongly disapproved of crabbing about the wind by anyone aboard my boat. I had turned to Robert Fitzgerald's translation of the *Odyssey* for comfort. I learned that in seagoing matters to do with sailing, Aeolus, even more than Poseidon, is the god to avoid offending. He's the Wind King, who can "rouse or calm at will," and that's a power that can influence a boat race.

So it has become ship routine, early on an offshore passage, to read aloud . . . the opening eighty-seven lines of Book Ten. It makes a fruitful ceremony of a happy hour to recite the visit of Odysseus and his shipmates to the island domain of Aeolus Hippotades. The tales of the Trojan War enthralled the host. To reward the doughty yarn-spinner, Aeolus provided Odysseus' ship, homebound for Ithaca, with "a bull's hide sewn from neck to tail into a mighty bag, bottling storm winds . . ."

> *He wedged this bag under my afterdeck,*
> *lashing the neck with shining silver wire*
> *so not a breath got through; only the west wind*
> *he lofted for me in a quartering breeze*
> *to take my squadron spanking home.*
> *No luck:*
> *the fair wind failed us when our prudence failed.*
> *Nine days and nights we sailed . . .*
> *but now, being weary to the bone, I fell*
> *into deep slumber . . .*

The crew believing the sack conceals "plunder out of Troy" which the skipper doesn't intend to share with them, untie the bag.

> *Then every wind*
> *roared into hurricane; . . .*
> *. . . the rough gale blew the ships*
> *and rueful crews clear back to Aiolia.*

This time our hero gets a cool welcome. "Why back again, Odysseus?" "What sea fiend rose in your path? Did we not launch you well / for home or for whatever land you chose?" The melancholy reply: "Mischief aboard and nodding at the tiller—a damned drowse— did for me." Says Aeolus:

> *"Take yourself out of this island, creeping thing—*
> *no law, no wisdom, lays it on me now*
> *to help a man the blessed gods detest—*
> *out!"* . . .
> *and comfortless we went again to sea,*
> *days of it, till the men flagged at the oars—*
> *no breeze, no help in sight* . . .

Could you ask for a more explicit warning to mariners? . . . At the end of the reading, I adjure my shipmates: "Please, aboard this vessel, never speak ill of the wind, no matter how much or how little. . . ." This is the Homeric Code as I read it.

"That's good," Tone says.

"But a little late," Chris says.

"Maybe we just got our comeuppance from Aeolus in advance. Now we know the code, maybe we're worthy of some decent wind? Or will you decide it's the woman and her bad luck and burn me at the mast?"

Chris stands by the mast. We sit aft of him on the house-roof. The steering wheel has tyrannized us all the way across. Now it is just another piece of lifeless gear. Who needs to drive if we're not going anywhere? No sails up, swaying somewhat, her hull reflected imperfectly in the sea, *Tresbelle* seems like a shapely platform, a house grown out of the water.

The barometer's up and still going up. Highs mean no wind. The BBC 2 "Scottish Fisheries" broadcast and the Nord Diech weather that I translated aren't zeroed in on where we are, but they both say "light and variable, becoming northwest."

"You know, Bels, as bent out of shape as we get after three days without wind—I mean, holding to the code—in the camps it must have been impossible. Years of it . . . it's amazing anybody held out at all."

"That's true."

"We can sit back and joke and maybe say kind things to

Aeolus," Tone says. "What was the the secret in the camps? How did any of you hold out?"

"I'm not sure there's a secret. I'm not even sure there's an answer."

But Tone persists. "I know it's a stupid question—and that most didn't hold out; they died. But I think it's what people want to know."

I guess you could say there were more or less two extremes. There was Ole, and a number of men like Ole, who held out so long only by withdrawing. Ole was tough, but the more time he spent in the camps the less he seemed to care about living. In Norway, in the sled dog club, Ole was decisive, a leader. He was always doing something for or with somebody else. What happened to Ole when he got to the camps amazed me. I still don't understand it. Everyone's different. He dealt with the camps his own way. I think it killed him, though. When the SS hassled us, most of us got mad. Thank God we did—it was better than being just helplessly scared. Ole never flared up; there was no fire in his eyes. He lost interest in eating, in warmth, in the others. He would sit by himself and stare most of the time. The closest I saw him to his old self was when he told us about the Warsaw uprising . . . what happened to his Polish friends. That was just about the last I saw of him. When the survivors of our group arrived later on in Dachau, they told me that he had stopped killing lice. Typhus got him. He was twenty-one years old.

Ian Hopper was the other extreme. He was British secret service, and that must have had a lot to do with it. He had worked in France since, I think, before the war started. He was at home with fighting. Whether he'd been trained so well or whether it was his temperament, or both, he was a fighter. When I think back, he was a sort of samurai. The samurai "live their own death," and I guess that's the beginning of courage, the source of their courage. And he was a zealot, like one of the early Christians or Moslems who believed death in battle was a passport to heaven. The janissaries, the Sultan's Guard, they all wore topknots so Allah would have something to grab hold of when he reached down to lift them to his bosom. Just like the soldiers of the cross, almost. Ian Hopper acted like that, he was that confident, that self-assured, that brave, but I don't think he was a bit religious. When the Allies finally liberated the camp, they set up a government by the prisoners. Ian was chosen to be second-in-command. He was reckless and crazy, but effective.

I guess most of the prisoners, myself included, fell somewhere between the two extremes of Ole and Ian. I made it, but it would have been so easy just to cave in . . . to sleep . . . to submit to the slings and arrows. Just close your eyes. I wanted to. Over and over again, I would ask myself, Why put up with this hunger, this disease and pain and filth and suffering? Why not just close my eyes?

But it amazed me how few prisoners gave in. I think I was somewhat typical. For me there were lots of reasons. Other people helped—my friends, other prisoners, lots of other desperate men. That made it harder to give up. Yet there were people like Jahren. He was a fighter, a zealot like Ian, but I saw death just overwhelm him. Nothing could have helped him. I was with him, trying to help him fight when he died.

Ian wrote to my sister after the war telling Sylvei about finding me with the decomposing bodies, over sixty dead in the "sick transport" to Dachau. He wrote, "Only because he fought so hard to live are you able to see him alive today." He never mentioned this to me, and it embarrasses me to talk of it, but I have to agree—the thing that kept me going was wanting to live. The sweeter life is in your nostrils, the longer you'll battle for breath. Life was sweet to me, and it still is. In some ways that saved me. It's hard to talk about these things.

Chapter Twenty

lready dead. A number with no name. I guess I was more than a little excited about sending a letter home from Dachau. A message from hell, a communiqué from beyond the edge. Whether the letter struck my family that way or not, they saved it. It is hardly an earthshaking letter. It is more the sort of letter that boys write home from camp, but when I look at the seals, the postmarks, the *"In deutscher Sprache"* stamp, the war eagle and swastika emblems that festoon it, and when I think of what it meant to break out of *Nacht und Nebel* anonymity to make contact, it was an important letter.

Dear family,

I am now in Dachau and everything is well with me. I think, of course, very often about you and hope that everything is well with you. I may now receive parcels from anybody. You can also send money. But do read the rules and regulations carefully, and when you write, it must be in German.

Send best regards to all my friends and a special greeting to Aunt Borghild.

Please send my address to Pastor Arne Berg at the Norwegian Sailors' Church in Hamburg.

Yours,
Arne

Aunt Borghild was the head of the Danish Red Cross. She had also been one of my mother's bridesmaids. For NN prisoners, especially, it was important to signal our whereabouts to the outside world. Arne Berg was a well-known Norwegian who spent the war in Hamburg. He was active helping prisoners, especially sailors, and he was one of the people who had the most to do with the Red Cross initiative to repatriate Scandinavian prisoners.

The Nazis kept no record of us. That's why my banal short letter probably had so much to do with finally getting home. No one could rescue us if we had disappeared.

We were still a long way from getting home. The Allies kept advancing and we heard news of Red Army victories, but we were still in Dachau where work made you free.

Our hospital at Dachau was good, good enough to save Juli-usen and me. It was also the center for the infamous experiments conducted on prisoners by Dr. Josef Mengele and his team.

The human-guinea-pig research in progress at Dachau had something to do with tropical warfare and determining how much quinine humans could ingest. At that time we heard only that being selected was the same as being sentenced to death. Ian routinely transcribed the list of selections. Twice I was on it. Twice he got me off.

I really didn't think very much about it at the time. I had such faith in Ian I just took it for granted. The second time we were discovered, though, and our cheating got us both expelled from the hospital into the main camp.

Ian, as I have said, had been in France for the British secret service before the war. His wife was French. In an ambush in Paris in 1942 his wife was shot and he was captured.

"I believe I hold a sort of world's record," he'd say. "Sixteen months chained hand and foot in Fresnes. They didn't kill me. I suppose they thought I was worth something to them. They did send me to Mauthausen—a good one to miss, old chap—and then Natzweiler, and now this lovely Bavarian resort."

Ian was fantastic. They had pulled most of his teeth and he had cigarette burns over his whole body, but he was the farthest thing from "broken." He lashed out at the guards and the capos. He even scared the SS. His habit was to shout at them, call them swine and tell them he would hang them all. "Yes, after the war . . . *schhwwwekkkk*"—with gestures and the sound effects of garotting he made sure the SS got his message. Then he would start into "God Save the King." Whether he knew they wouldn't kill him or just didn't care, he was incredible. With Ian around it was easy to be damn near as brave as he was.

There were twelve English secret service men in Dachau, and an RN chap, Pat O'Leary, was their leader. They more or less adopted me. One of my first impressions of the group was that they were extraordinarily musical. I thought that it might be simple homesickness or morale-boosting. At any rate, every day we struck up songfests: "Tipperary," "Sweet Molly Malone," "Oh, Dear, What Can the Matter Be?" and all of the standards. The guards were used to it—crazy Englishmen, they thought—and it became a sort of rallying point for prisoners. After the war, though, I learned we were just a distraction used to shield the "White Rabbit," the secret organization inside Dachau that had a hidden radio transmitter and coordinated escapes for selected prisoners who were smuggled out of Germany to Italy and picked up by submarines.

Dachau was a kingpin in the Nazi *Konzentrationslager* system, and it was almost equally distant from Eastern and Western fronts. That was why the Reich chose it as a depository for prisoners from all over, and our camp brimmed full as the Allies and the Red Army each pushed waves of prisoners toward it.

There were two, three, often four of us in every bed. The food situation deteriorated. For a while we had no salt. Even the hungriest of us had trouble eating the watery soup without salt. "The salt of life" had been just an expression. Now I understood it. Ian's job of recording new arrivals from the transports became full-time. A transport came from Dautmergen. I went to see the prisoners in the arrival pen. There was Ragnvald.

He was bent and slow. There was no life at all in his eyes, but he was alive. Ole? Erik? Of our sixteen-man group from Grini, I knew of only five still alive. There was an alley splitting the camp in two. I walked Ragnvald down it to our barracks. The three-minute walk took us almost twenty minutes. He looked as though he had nothing left. No smile. I waited, hoping he would wink at me, but he didn't.

"Ole?"

"He gave up. He stopped picking lice. The typhus ate him up."

"Erik?"

"Lost track of him, but learned that he also died of typhus."

"The rest?"

"What you see." Which was six other Norwegians, two of whom had been in Natzweiler when we arrived.

Once again Ian was fantastic. Despite the overcrowding in the hospital, he got Ragnvald a bed. My friends had arrived at a terrible time in Dachau. There had always, veterans said, been lice. Now people started dying. They had high fevers,

nd if you pinched the skin it left a sort of black mark. The
ice and the typhus were only in one half of the camp. The
5D closed off the other half, and anyone new was added to
our diseased half.

We knew that the lice brought typhus, but there were other
pests that took up our daily routine. There was scabies—a par-
asite that gets under the skin. They're very much like crabs.
Everybody had them. They itched like crazy, especially when
you settled into bed and they started to migrate toward warm
spots. Fleas were not so much of a threat, but they were everywhere. Ragnvald established a new Bavarian off-season record
by killing thirty-two fleas in his socks. And then there were
larger insects, I don't really know what they were. They
reminded me of ticks, but they didn't have pointy little heads
like ticks. They would mostly drop on us from the ceiling at
night.

Lice, though, were the real killers. If you wanted to live,
you had to kill lice. It was a full-time occupation. They were
yellow, almost transparent. The big ones weren't that hard to
catch and crush between your nails. But they laid eggs, usually
in the seams of your uniform. It was disgusting to have your
body nibbled and ruled by these crawling things. And we could
do so little about it. It was as though we truly were already
dead.

Dachau grew worse every day. The SD all but abandoned
us. They brought food to the gate. The barracks and toilets
were left to overflow. More people came every day. Overcrowding was our worst enemy, more lethal than starvation or
disease. We trampled and elbowed one another. Everywhere
people died.

Typhus was a plague. The Black Death of the Middle Ages
could not have been worse. We hunted lice around the clock,
but new people came, new disease, and it was a disaster. The
lice carried the disease. It caused a high fever, around 105
degrees Fahrenheit, for a week or ten days. At the end of that

time one was either alive or dead. The doctors, even the Dacha
doctors, had rarely seen typhus and knew nothing about it
They just let it run its course, and it ran. People in good health
have a 90 percent mortality rate. Chances were much wors
for us already dead.

In January and February of 1945, sixteen thousand peopl
died in Dachau, most of them in our half of the camp. Ther
was no coal, so they had no way to burn the bodies. Wood
stacks of corpses proliferated. Limbs like stiffened ganglia poke
in jarring ways at raw angles out of the body piles. No one die
easily in Dachau, and no one even lay easily. They dragge
bodies out the barracks doors in the morning. Heads of th
corpses bounced sickeningly on the stairs. Ragnvald and
laughed. Now they made us load the hand-pulled carts. On
took the hands, one the legs, then a swing and a thump,
sound like in a slaughter house, as if we were loading sides o
beef.

Seen from a distance, when we could get that far away from
them, the body stacks looked something like dinosaur skele
tons. They surely weren't piles of flesh. Then, in the middl
of the broken muddle of anonymous bones, you couldn't hel
but see faces—gaping, grimacing, wide-eyed faces, faces tha
destroyed all symmetry, all metaphor, all defenses.

Ian, Ragnvald, and I all got typhus. I can't remember much
The worst was when I was delirious and wandered off by mysel
to the toilet. The barracks were all lit with blue lights for air
raid blackouts. I woke to find myself shivering in the toile
room. In front of me was a massive pile of corpses. All I coul
see was an endless wall of corpses. I cycled between flashes o
clarity and waves of gauzy hallucination. I was bombarded b
blue . . . blue glints off teeth, blue glows in eyes, the blu
wash over dull, stiff flesh. It looked like snow . . . they wer
snowmen. Skinny snowmen. Where was the campfire? Wer
my dogs tied well? Noses jutting like clothespins cast shadow
like small pines on teeth jutting like headlands, tiny blu

eadlands, so bare to the air, cold, bone cold . . . holes in
heir heads . . . heads full of holes.

No wonder they're dead, I thought. Their souls came out
hose holes. Isn't there anything else? Life's turned to stone
. . to bone, to indigo grins, to blue-tiled eyes. Isn't anything
eft? Anyone? . . . Get a grip, if I can just think, yes . . . but
can't get under the corpses. No way around them. God, this
nust be a dream . . . make this please be a dream. I'm okay.
Now I'm fine . . . but why am I screaming? Shut up, clench
ight, choke yourself . . . don't scream. Don't *scream*.

More startling even than my prison of corpses was the prisoner. Gaunt, tall, black-eyed even in the blue light, he keened
nd rocked on the hard tile floor of the *Scheisserei*. Hidden
rom me till I rounded a corner of the corpse pile, the man
ave out wail after wail of piercing animal terror, of panting,
hoking fright. One effect of the screams was to shake my own
allucinations into the background. Caught in the same death
rap, he kept screaming while I kept trying to silence him.
Someone finally came and took us both away.

Not long after that my fever broke. I experienced black spots
efore my eyes and strange noises in my ears, common after-
ffects of typhus. But none stayed with me as long nor shook
ne so deeply as the blue-black nightmares of the charnel toilet.

Things had gone to hell in Dachau so completely that Ian
ecided the only way to survive was to escape. Escapes were
lmost unheard-of. But Ian was Ian, and he had a gun! He
vouldn't tell me where he'd gotten it, but while the rest of us
ad little more than wooden spoons, he had a gun. It was an
ld-fashioned revolver. His cartridges—he had five—were too
mall to fit the chamber snugly, so he just wrapped them with
aper until they did.

Spring was coming. If we were going to escape, we needed
o be fit. We marched up and down outside our barracks as
nuch as we could without calling attention to ourselves.
Actually, in the chaotic world of late-war Dachau, two ener-

getic marchers were hardly a top worry for the SS.

By March, though, we scrubbed our escape plans. Ian heard, via the secret wireless, that prisoners would be sent to Switzerland through the Red Cross. At last, at bloody long last! But we'd been expecting to see the Allies breaking down the camp gates for months. Even a rumor on such good authority was still a rumor. We'd believe it when we saw the Alps.

While we were waiting, the SD had a final laugh. Our barracks had at last been put off quarantine. (Everyone in our half of the camp had undoubtedly already had typhus.) We were to police our area for the grand SS inspection. The guards stomped in. I don't know why, but Ragnvald was bent over probably pushing something underneath his bed. The first guard said nothing, just went up behind Ragnvald and kicked him square in the spine with his boot. It was a toe-pointed kick the way you'd drive a free kick toward the goal in soccer. I was surprised I didn't hear Ragnvald's spine crack. He went face down on the floor in spasms. The guards told us to get him up. He was sobbing and retching and twitching, but the sons of bitches made us hold him at attention through the whole thing. Ragnvald was badly hurt, but there was no room in the infirmary. He kept saying, "It's better than the leg," and he got so he could deal with the pain whenever he didn't have to move much. We did our best to keep the guards from trying to work him into further agony. He began to heal.

The Allies approached, and it became clearer there was no way the Reich could salvage victory. How would the friendly SD take that frustration out? Ian was excited. He learned that Count Bernadotte and the Swedish Red Cross would be taking care of all Scandinavian prisoners. The Nazis would let them. They would come to Dachau? All but the NN, I worried. We wouldn't have put it past them to take the NN prisoners out and hang them.

The following two weeks were full of building tension shot with rumor. Tension about the evacuation. Could it be real

That simple? Tension every time more than one guard approached. Plus two weeks of trying, in the same old way, to stay alive. No one wanted to die in the last week of the war.

One day they called all Scandinavian prisoners to Dachau's *Appellplatz*. Not just Scandinavian NN prisoners—a good sign. Not just a small enough group to be transported into oblivion. There were six hundred policemen from Copenhagen. They'd been in Dachau only a few weeks. It was reassuring to have them thrown in with the night and fog already dead. I suppose there was nothing to prevent them from executing the policemen, too, but even I found that somehow hard to believe.

There on the *Appellplatz* the SS joked and kidded with us! They gave us clean clothes! It couldn't be real. It had to be a fairy tale. The same guards who beat and terrorized us, the same SS who helped at hangings and hit us across the face with crops . . . were joking with us? It was one of the strangest events in my time in the camps. It didn't last long.

The camp gates opened. No tanks. No greasy transport trucks. Buses. A fleet of buses. Great white Red Cross buses, with Swedish flags painted on them. I do not know how many they were. All of them white, and they came right into the camp and drew up between the block buildings. The cypress trees always looked somehow artificial. Then they began to look real. The white buses made them blossom into real trees.

So this was it? This was real? What was the trick? Son of a bitch, life . . . there really was such a thing?

There were tears on Ragnvald's cheeks. Stooped forward, unable to straighten, he smiled across the rows at me. Through my tears I could just make him out. It was what I'd dreamed of for a year. God, what a year. Choked with feeling, throat and chest, I finally believed this was happening. Like white elephants the buses had broken down those gates. They had beaten the barbed wire and shooed off the dogs and defanged the guards. Those beautiful buses.

Nurses. Women . . . well-fed, with curves, and clean . . . *nurses*.

They put the people in stretchers on first. We were going to a camp near Hamburg. We were going to be protected now by the Swedish Red Cross. Capos? "Selections"? *Appellplatz*? Medical experiments? No more. *No more!* Oh, Lord!

Finally we boarded the buses. There was one Gestapo guard on each. And then we just rolled through the Dachau gates. That was all there was to it. We just rode out.

Excited, exhausted, speeding out from under death-tension, most of us promptly fell asleep. The lurch of the bus and screech of brakes woke me—just as we hit a tree. My first thought was that the dream bubble had popped. A trick? A trap? A sweet nightmare?

The driver, it seemed, had dozed off too. At any rate, we wandered off the road into the tree. No one was hurt but the Gestapo guard. Providence . . . the beginning of revenge? Then I was surprised. A nurse and even some prisoners went to help the guard. Then it came to me. This was a new world . . . the civilized world.

Chapter Twenty-one

I bounced clear off my bed. Bomb blasts as close together as machine-gun fire jostled me into the air. I was held there between gravity and flight. My eyeballs felt pressed into my head. My lungs stopped working. Express trains of falling bombs rolled right over me. Pounding flashes, splitting crashes, earthquake eruptions, volcano blasts of light and heat. But I wasn't scared.

I had made it this far. No air raid, not even the worst one of my life, could get me now. I did, however, take the precaution of diving under my bed. So this was what they'd rescued us into?

At Neuengamme, near Hamburg, under Red Cross auspices, we were bombed harder than ever before in the war, but otherwise the camp was like heaven: food, more than we'd seen in a year was laid out for us that week. The guards were only a few Germans, and they seemed scared now. Even the bunks were a treat. Solitary sleeping . . . imagine!

There we joined seven hundred Norwegian students, the famous victims of the Nazification in Norway who were hauled from their classrooms one day in 1943. The Nazis simply encircled the university and rounded up all of its students . . . *because they were students!* Freedom of thought and the academic traditions were barriers, thought Quisling and Jonas Lie— barriers to the new order. But that mass arrest was even more than an attack on the university. The Nazis were trying to turn students into Judas goats, trying to force into existence an elite that would lead the bulk of Norwegians into Nazism, as the Nazis themselves had failed to do. Some of the students were permitted to continue their studies, and all were given relatively easy treatment in the camps, and through it all the Nazis persistently tried to seduce the students into "enlistment" in the Waffen SS. There was much made of the Aryan ties between our peoples, the need for a natural elite, the opportunity to shape the future. Not a single student enlisted. Not a goddam one. We were proud to learn that.

When we were joined with the students, our NN status was erased. Students to the core, Ragnvald and I joked about the "tough course" that we'd had, but we were more than happy to exchange our already-dead identities for student IDs. A ninety-pound stork and his stooped, nearly toothless, limping companion, Ragnvald and I, heads shaven, faces drawn, were a strange pair to be coming home for midterm break.

We'd heard the growl of big guns in the distance before. Now it was Montgomery's Eighth Army driving across the top of Germany. We were between them and the Germans, and that hastened our departure from camp. Neuengamme too had been a concentration camp and was known for its gas chamber. As we stood on its *Appellplatz*, we were almost as glad to leave as we had been to march out of Natzweiler or ride away from Dautmergen or see the Dachau gates open for the great white fleet of buses. Even though we had been fed well, even eggs, the place was all too familiar to us.

Ten thousand Scandinavians, we stood mustered there on the *Appellplatz*, waiting for Red Cross buses. The roar of guns was intermittent, but around us now we saw squadrons of Spitfires. Secure beneath the Red Cross banners flying over the camp, we watched the British fighters dive and strafe targets on the rivers and roads around the camp. No one took cover . . . such was our faith in the Red Cross flag and the men above who understood it.

I don't know why, but I waited. When the buses came I was the next-to-last person to board. Courage from the Resistance fighter who dropped his pamphlets in the garbage can? Bravado like that of the little boy who ran through the Nazi tank park in Oslo? I don't know, but after the war I met at a party one of the pilots who'd flown a Spitfire over Hamburg. He was Norwegian—it was a Norwegian squadron, escaped pilots trained in England, strafing that day.

"The Red Cross flags got so they didn't mean a thing. The Nazis used them on all sorts of military targets. To be effective at all, we found we had to ignore them," he told me.

The buses stopped not far from Hamburg that night. There was shelling over a ridge behind us, so we moved on. I was drowsing. When I woke again we were in the middle of an inferno. It was the town of Lübeck. There must have been a firebomb raid. Flames were everywhere. As we drove through, safe in our speeding buses and fresh from our own versions of hell, it felt as though this were a blurred and scratchy movie being shown out of focus. It was hard to connect at all with the destruction outside. It seemed half real, remote. We stopped. There was a commotion in front of us. One of the buses had hit someone. A little girl. She was dead.

Early the next morning we crossed the Danish border. Out of Germany . . . out of the Rhineland and back to Scandinavia. That was a milestone, but I had trouble staying awake while we were waiting for the border guards. We stopped at Frøslev, a concentration camp in Denmark now run by the

Red Cross. The prisoners formed ranks. Ten thousand of us.
Red Cross officials inspected and counted us. It was different
from the *Appellplatz* . . . no drill, no prods, no corpses falling
to the ground. Near me was a team of nurses. She was one of
them.

"Bente?"

She turned around.

"Bente? Is that you, Bente?"

"Yes . . ."

She didn't recognize me.

"It's me . . . Arne."

"Arne?"

"Arne Lie."

Now *she* was flabbergasted. We hadn't seen each other since
before the war. Bente was Aunt Borghild's daughter. We had
played together on the Hardangerfjord in the summers when
we were kids growing up. And here she was, a nurse with the
Danish Red Cross.

"My God. Arne. Arne!"

She gave me a big hug. I think we both cried a bit. I know
for certain that I did. It was hard to speak. All I could think
was that this was perfect; this was what a homecoming should
be.

Beyond the hugs it was hard to know what to say.

"You've been in the camps?"

"Yes. Dachau. Natzweiler and Dautmergen before that. For
a year."

"Oh, Arne. You're not sick?"

"I don't think so, no more than anyone else. Could you
perhaps call my parents? Tell them I'm all right and I'm coming home. Tell them I'm okay."

"Oh, Arne, don't worry. Don't worry. I will, of course. I
will. Safe trip."

Imagine that. "Safe trip." There really was a civilized world
left!

The buses continued. Up the Jutland Peninsula over wind-
ing country roads. Our bus stopped at a farm for the night.
They let us out to sleep in the hay. The farmer cooked big
slabs of ham for us in the morning, gave us eggs and coffee,
and when we went to get back on the buses our German guards
were gone. Another milestone to freedom! Since the Stapo
had broken into my apartment and taken me from my bedroom, I had been controlled by the Nazis. Today a deep breath
of free air.

I felt drained, more exhausted than I could remember. The
food, the freedom, the meeting with Bente . . . they wore me
out. I felt like a wet rag almost all of the time. Who knew what
it would take to get a zest for life back? I had trouble staying
awake on the ride to Copenhagen. I'd try to snap awake to see
where we were, to talk with someone, but within a minute or
two I'd be nodding. I couldn't make anything focus. All that
mattered was sleep. Ragnvald and I sat together most of the
time. He was quiet, very quiet. I don't think he slept that much,
for his back gave him constant pain. Every time I woke up, he
was awake. We both laughed when it seemed appropriate to
laugh, we were happy to be alive, but there was no exuberance
in our coming back. Ragnvald smoldered and I drowsed and
the buses drove toward Copenhagen.

The buses arrived at quayside shortly before noon. By one
o'clock our ferry was full; before two o'clock we were in Sweden. Free. It was precise, surgical. In fact, it felt something
like a razor cut or maybe a paper cut: thin, not too deep, even
hard to find. I had expected an emotional watershed when I
crossed the Skagerrak from Nazi-occupied Denmark to neutral
Sweden. It was funny. Freedom seemed just to scratch my
feelings and not really touch them.

We weren't technically free, actually, for another ten days.
The Red Cross quarantined us. The quarantine was pretty much
of a formality, though. We were in a hotel. We could come
and go as we liked. We were given new clothes, snappy and

louseless. Plus a cardboard suitcase. What did we have to put
in it? No one had saved his prison rags. I saved my Dachau
number, though, just the cloth panel.

They deloused us, and we were issued new Norwegian pass-
ports. It was sweet to have my name back.

Somewhere in there came V-E Day. The final Allied victory in Europe. You see pictures of dancing and champagne
and wild celebrating. In Sweden, it was just another day. We
gave each other a restrained thumbs-up or two. I had first felt
victory when the first SS—actually, the second; I didn't know
what to make of the first—smiled and joked with me on the
Appellplatz in Dachau. The bastards had been kings, had been
slave drivers, had been anything but human the whole year I
was under arrest. When they started acting human, even if it
was to save their own skins, even if it was to try to cover up for
all of the atrocities they had in their closet, that was the real
end of the war for me. A separate peace?

After quarantine they made us wait for transport. There were
no complaints. We were used to waiting. The things we dreamed
about when we were behind barbed wire—food, drink, women,
freedom to move, warmth, comfort—were all there in Mölle,
the little seaside town where we waited in Sweden.

The discovery that those things couldn't put our Humpty
Dumpty lives back together again came hard to me. I didn't
know what to make of it, but I had no interest in or energy for
virtually anything. I felt half alive. From already dead to half
alive might be the right direction, but where were the wings I
thought would take my soul when I was free?

And then the bugle blew and we were on a train home. It
was a ten-hour ride, about. We drank for most of those hours.
Aquavit and ale. That's what you did when you came home
from the war, wasn't it? Drink. I guess we were wondering
what kind of welcome we'd get in Oslo. I didn't think they'd

pin medals on us for crushing lice or for shitting in our pants
ten times a day. I guess we were wondering how we'd tell our
families, what close friends we had left, about the camps. How
could they understand? It seems ironic, but coming home I
was scared. Had the camps made me an outcast from my own
family? Had what happened to me set me on an island that no
one else could ever get to?

We entered the outskirts of Oslo, and you could feel the
excitement . . . the mix of anticipation, hope, and fear. I had
been sleeping on the baggage shelf. My silly cardboard suitcase
at the ready, I was straining toward the station. Toward what?
Homecoming. What home did I have now? Who would I find
at home? Familiar landmarks, unfamiliar feelings . . . heart
pumping, sawdust sifting . . . Mother, Father, Kirsten, Sylvei . . .

And here we are. We've all been down these tracks before.
We all recognize old-time spots, funny things we didn't know
we'd recognize. The shops are still almost empty of goods,
people's clothes are old and worn-out, but there are Norwegian flags, beautiful flags, *everywhere!* I feel lucky and tired
and sad and tired and happy and tired. Some people on the
train slap each other, pointing and laughing. None of us from
the NN camps seem to feel that way. Tore and I are the only
ones to weep. We're here!

In the station we form in ranks. The Red Cross is shepherd-
ing us. The ranks are ragged, no hint at all of *ein, zwei, drei,
vier, fünf.* Loosely formed, we march out of the station. There
are people on either side of the street. Some turn and follow
our procession as we go by. Our cardboard suitcases feel as
irrelevant and are as empty as our camp berets. "Suitcases *auf!*"

It's a glorious May day in Oslo. The feel and smell of the
streets is friendly, is comforting. As awful as I feel, this is my
city. Sometimes people gawk. They did that in Denmark and

Sweden, too. They've seen scarecrows before, but not ones with cardboard suitcases, shaved heads, and sunken eyes. I hear "Welcome" and "Well done" in choruses on either side. "Congratulations." V for victory, for the king. These signs and shouts pop up here and there. There is no real cheering, though. People tend to be taken aback rather than moved to cheer when they see us. But our welcome feels warm.

Primarily they've come to welcome the students home. I wonder how many student corpses they stacked in student morgues, how many students fell rattling dead over their books. What the hell, I thought, don't be petty and embarrass yourself. The students had it tough enough, tougher than anyone should have it. We all had it tough.

We march up Karl Johans Gate, the main street of Oslo. There's a small plaza in front of the university. We assemble there. There is a small stand. A man mounts it and speaks to us. He is the dean of the university. Even though some of us look haunted, thin, sunken-eyed, he addresses us all as students. The return of the students is the "real victory." The loyalty and bravery of Norway's young men is clear in these before us, here is the victory of man's right to think and question and learn over the forces that would grind thought down.

I am moved and depressed. The students are a good lot, and they did well. What we faced and did isn't so easy to talk about. I wonder what I will talk about to my parents.

We are released, handed over to our families, and I go home. They help me home. I try to be polite. I try to talk and eat the favorite sweets they have ready for me. I try even to cover some parts of the year that has passed. But I find myself losing my words in midsentence, falling out of touch with people right while they're talking to me.

"It was really a long train ride. I think I'd better go to bed." And with quick, abashed good nights I retire to my room, the room where the *ta-pok-ka-pok* of the Stapo van woke me just over a year ago.

Chapter Twenty-two

There was water everywhere, flat water. Our fourth day of doldrums! Still not a drop of wind. Drifting . . . not really drifting, because drifting is moving . . . sitting in the North Atlantic, 450 miles now from Ireland. We were caught. Caught with an engine with a mind of its own, a shorted, sizzling electrical system. It was hot under the cloudless sky. Too hot really even to continue keeping everything shipshape. We slept, we talked, we read. In a way it was pleasant. Once I stopped being frantic about getting home, about seeing Ellen again, it was much easier.

After lunch and a siesta, Chris and I dove into the engine again. We still didn't know what was wrong, but with a stable platform and good drying weather, we figured we'd lay it all out carefully and get it dried out. After an hour of bending and swearing around the engine we emerged, sweat-covered and greasy, not much more certain that it would work.

We knew the ocean would be cold, but we rigged rope ladders and plunged. Yow! We hung from the ropes over the side and did our deep-sea cleansing with Joy dish detergent, miraculous for sudsing in salt water. We hadn't seen a shark in three days, and we'd seen only one pod of killer whales, but thoughts of such company became larger and larger in my head when I took a few strokes away from the boat. There's no logic to the fear, I know, but nonetheless my instincts tell me man was not meant to thrash about on the surface of a miles-deep pool filled with hungry things bigger than he is. I took three quick strokes back to the rope. On the second stroke the old Natzweiler maxim, "We wash you, then we kill you," flashed comfortingly into my brain. I was up the rope and in the cockpit with embarrassing speed.

By evening it was cool enough to cook. Sipping a warm Watney's, half of which I added to the pot, I steamed some tinned shrimp and made a curry, using our dried apples, nuts, raisins, and enough curry powder to be a suitable antidote to the polar heat wave we were experiencing, and we had the meal in the cockpit with some more of our estimable *rouge*. By now it had almost ceased to amaze Chris how well the red Bordeaux tastes with the fishes of the sea.

It must have been midnight when I stumbled topside to take a leak. Chris and Tone were still up. I stumbled past them with what *politesse* I could muster and, somewhat sleepily, somewhat urgently, leaned against the stern rail and urinated into the sea. At first I thought I saw phosphorescence. Sparks seemed to dance in front of me on the water where my stream splatted. But it was weaker, more ancient light. It was the stars. I was well awake now. I could see. The stars were reflected in the table-flat water underneath the stern. Ink with fireflies floating, the ocean was absolutely flat. I thought about those strange paper-cup lighthouses we'd loosed with the garbage the other night—those cups could still be standing tall in the middle of the dreaded Atlantic. The polished black mirror beneath me seemed so smooth I felt I was pissing into the sky, sending my silly stream back up the starbeams.

"This is fantastic!" I said to myself.

"Have you ever been in a starbowl like this before?" Tone called aft to me.

"No, I've never seen the sea like this."

The cloudless sky, the flat sea, the clear ocean air—they made it impossible to tell where the stars in the sky left off and those in the sea began. It was eerie and beautiful, as if we were hanging in the middle of a midnight birdcage.

"We were going to wake you, but we got talking," Chris said.

"*I* wanted to call you but *he* got talking," said Tone.

"Yeah, well, I just thought this made a super planetarium. What better way for Mademoiselle Cabdriver to pick up some of the navigational pointers she's always whining for when I'm trying to take a sight in six-foot seas? A guided tour of the lighthouses in the sky."

"I was looking for constellations when this pushy gent started waving his astrolabe under my nose and saying he was going to make me a star."

I had to laugh at Chris and Tone. I was glad they were kinder to their old skipper than they were to each other.

"That reddish one . . . look, you can see it in both the sky and the sea," I said. "Mars?"

"Mars? The star of war?" Tone asked.

"The god of war," Chris corrected.

"You pedantic jerk. Why do you have to spoil something this beautiful by being such a picky ass?" Tone exploded.

"If you could see, if you had the discipline to see things the way they are, if you'd give your goddam silly fantasies a rest every now and then, maybe you'd be doing something more than pushing a cab around all your life."

I wondered if it was just the stars that had them so upset.

"When you look up from your goddam navigation tables, you'll see reality . . . you'll see that you're compulsive and cranky and tight-assed and that you're all alone. All alone, just you and your index cards on life." Tone stood up. "Looking at

this through your piggy little eyes isn't any fun for me. . . .
Sorry, Bels. Good night." She went below.

We squirmed there awhile in the silent dark.

"No trouble getting a sight tonight. No horizon now, but it
must have been good at twilight, for Betelgeuse."

"Thanks, Bels, thanks a hell of a lot. I've been busting my
ass with all of this ratshit no-good electronics and no steerer
and no sights and fog and waves and all you keep doing is
bugging me."

"I'm sorry. No. I just . . . I know it's been tough to navi-
gate. You've done a hell of a job. Much better than I could
have."

"I don't know. I mean, I—"

"Chris, I was trying to make a joke to say somehow how
much I . . . how much we depend on you."

"Thanks. . . . Maybe the queen has cooled down. Maybe I
should go down. Good night."

Our happy ship. Chris has gone below, and I sit in the cockpit thinking about our happy ship and how bad her skipper just
was at handling one of his best shipmates ever. But then there's
the big picture. No wind, no power, tempers snapping left and
right, another three days maybe to landfall. But there are stars
in the sky, and in the sea. There's Bordeaux still, and even
food. And these kids have been great and the trip has been
great. I guess.

Mars. Out of all of those stars, why did I pick the war one?
Or does it matter? This feels like a chintzy dancehall now . . .
little white lightpricks on the ceiling and floor. Like droplets
of dried toothpaste or birdshit or . . . an empty dance hall.
And up there ahead somewhere is Oslo. My "home." Starlight
and birdshit, birdshit and starlight . . . at least I think I can
tell the difference. Mumble mumble . . . what kind of sense
do you make of it all, Bels? Your happy ship, your gallant

rew, your normal life, your noble cause? But these stars aren't
pinpricks on a dancehall wall. They're so big and old and divine
they wipe you out, they take "sense" away . . . or do they give
it? Listen to me whistle. Am I whistling? Whistling for a wind?
Only fools and witches whistle at sea. Which are thee?" When
have fears that I have ceased to be . . .

I crawl into my quarterberth to get out of the starlight.

Tiny Tot is drawing nicely, heating well. Even though it's
noon, Chris couldn't see the sun for a sight through this glug
if it were trying to land on the masthead. There is rain spitting
at us from huge gray clouds all around. Just twelve hours ago
the world was a star bowl. We're moving, though. It's nasty
out, but a southeast breeze is better than an easterly, and we're
not drifting or beating our brains out. We're close-reaching,
making better than six knots. I'll take it.

I'm nestled up against the port settee, right aft of Tiny Tot.
I'm trying to catch up with the log:

>August 8
>[in Chris's hand]
>1500   065 making 7 knots in steady easterly.
>1600   Wind more on the nose . . . 6.2 for the hour.
>1700   Wind lighter 5 knot average—065.
>1800   Wind very light . . . would set drifter if we had one
>   . . . 4 knots made good on course.
>
>[Tone]
>1830   Hard to tell where he comes up with the ingredients
>   . . . not Beef Wellington, exactly, but Bels Welling-
>   ton, I guess. Who would have thought canned bully
>   beef would taste like that . . . a "puff" that really
>   poufed . . . some *vin rouges* . . . *quelle fête*.
>1900   Still coming down, calming down from dinner. Good

thing there's not too much sailing to be done in thi
light air. You can get an extra half-knot, though
driving off in the puffs and riding up again in the
lulls. I keep telling that to Chris.

2000   Strange mountain of clouds, an anvilhead almost bu
[and she drew a picture]. As the wet-behind-the-ear
weather girl I guess I just have to observe these thing
and record what happens. What will the Book say,
wonder?

2100   The book says, "This shape due to violent updrafts.
It's *cumulonimbus*. "Winds are strong around these
threatening clouds." This one turned golden, then
white, puffed up, and didn't move much. I would
almost say the anvil became a mound. The breeze
lightened and veered from the east into the south
Then it went away.

2200   Confused by the book . . . seems to suggest more
wind coming . . . we've got less. Book says change
of shape was from cumulonimbus to cumulus . .
fair-weather sign . . . revoltingly fair.

Why is it always up to me to put the indescribables into the
log book? Our "official record" shouldn't leave it out, but I'l
be damned if I know how to describe that star show.

August 11

0000   Three of us unable to sleep. We sat and talked in a
bowl of stars. Reflections and stars surrounded us
The walrus said the time had come and we talked o
many things.

0400   Solitary thinking on the edge of the star pool.

This kind of sailing is *Tresbelle's* meat. Close-reaching, twenty
knots of breeze. We have the staysail and yankee up, a "double
head rig." It's a sail combination to rhapsodize about. The

glorious cutter rig lets you have two jibs up at the same time, and when the breeze is fresh and the seas are lumping . . . oh, there's no better way to make miles. Power with control with efficiency with minimal strain on rig, boat, crew. I'm not bashful about it . . . I'm a cutter man, and I'll argue for the double head rig.

I wonder what Sigurd will say when we tie up again in his yard. Two transatlantics, a great TwoStar result . . . but Sigurd is always the jujitsu master, always on balance and throwing you off. He'll probably tell me the reason Gus and Toffen didn't win the TwoStar was the extra foot on *Tresbelle*'s bow. "All that increased pitching moment. Should have known you would put too much strain on the head stay." Old prick that he is, I'm still anxious to see him. Maybe from Oban we should bring him some haggis.

We have begun using the AM broadcasts on the BBC to try for rough lines of position. The limeys do talk funny, don't y'know. Chris is concentrating on working the radio direction finder antenna to get a "null" when they play a fine Irish reel.

"Don't tune that out!" I shout at him, and I try to get him to dance a bit of a jig. There's something very spiritual in an old man returning to the Old World, but Chris puts me back in a soberer mood. He finally comes up with a position. He makes it sound as though the exact coordinates were whispered to him by Prince Henry the Navigator's ghost . . . 364 miles to the canal, 244 to Arran Island at the corner where we enter the Irish Sea. "Three days to go."

I like cooking in a breeze. Take dried fish *gratiné à l'ail*. I soak the fish for forty-eight hours in seawater. Hake, pollock, halibut, cod, just about any fish will fit this recipe. Then I drain the fish. On top of it I make mashed potatoes, to which I add five garlic cloves (peeled), olive oil, milk powder, water, and salt and pepper. I bake in a medium oven and decorate with black olives. This is a great meal to cook underway because you can do it all in one pot, and because you don't have to cook anything except the mashed potatoes before you cook the whole.

We take turns eating, then I go on watch.

It has been unfortunate not to have a self-steerer for this trip. We've all had to work a lot harder than we should. Now, too little and too late, I've arranged a little self-steering system of my own. I lead a line from the self-steerer's steering arm forward. I can sit tucked out of rain and spray and tug at it from the shelter of the canvas dodger. The boat now, double headsails up and close-reaching, very nearly steers herself.

A landfall. Our landfall on Ireland, any landfall, for better and worse, is the end of being at sea. It's the proof of the passage, it's the test of the navigator. "Where are we?" is no open question anymore. If you know where you are, you know where to go. If you don't you have to flounder and guess.

This is no easy landfall. The currents run diagonally across our approach, and that makes calculating sideward drift very tricky. They run at up to two knots, and they run stronger in one direction than they do the other. That takes lots of figuring or a superior nose for rocks in the fog. Just before breakfast, Chris picked up Eagle Island Radio—range 100 miles. That puts us 140 miles from Tory Island. A day's jump, then another 120 across Oban and the mouth of the canal. This trip is flying by.

Tucked under the dodger, I think about a time back in 1979 when I took *Tresbelle* to the Amsterdam Boat Show. It was February. Chris came with me, and also Steff Herbern, Sigurd's son, and Erling Brunborg (whose brother died in Natzweiler).

The four of us . . . February or not. The Skagerrak was damn near impassable with ice floes. We picked our way through. In the North Sea it was sleeting, out of the southwest. No visibility. The rigging kept icing up, then the deck; the waves were building. Blowing thirty . . . each snow squall harder than the last. Whether or not we could have made it, none of us was anxious to keep slogging to the Ijsselmeer. So we made for Helgoland. It's not a big harbor. I wondered how we'd find the channel through the breakers. I had an idea of our position, but we were looking for buoys surrounded by surf.

Following the ten-fathom curve, we powered south with just the storm jib set. Out of the sleet to leeward we saw a ship . . . a pair of fishing boats, actually. Danish trawlers. These guys fished out here all winter. They would know what they were up to. I radioed. Could they give us their position? With the mike open the skipper yelled, "Where the hell are we?" Voices thick with schnapps argued, but they couldn't agree, so we left them to ride out the storm.

We broke ice again, clubbing the lower rigging and lifelines, parts of the deck. Chris was ready to search for the sea buoy off Helgoland and find the channel mouth from there. I tried looking for another angle. I radioed the captain of the port at Helgoland, told him how tired we were, how tough the visibility had become. I asked if he might switch on his radar and give us some guidance to get in.

"Don't worry. I'll come out and lead you in."

Half an hour after those welcome words we saw his powerful eighty-five-foot rescue vessel, twin screws and a high, centerline bridge, through the sleet. The captain, a ruddy young guy and a hell of a seaman, came aboard *Tresbelle* with his crew after we tied up. Eight fit snugly around our table. We had nothing to serve except the moonshine that I make, but, using German, English, Norwegian, and snippets of French, we found words and more in common in the midst of the blizzard.

Blueberry pancakes—Tone and I collaborate. A good start to our twenty-second day at sea. Even though it's bumpy, this kind of close-reaching into the seas always helps me sleep. The jolts are predictable. It's been three days since we've had a sun sight . . . no stars either. The DR and the RDF are all Chris can use.

Scrambled eggs. We're getting close. We're all aware, though, on this twenty-third day at sea, that we have a rugged landfall in front of us. It would be nice to have the loran C, but it went on the blink leaving Boston. While my Viking heart beats faster to be coming out of the North Sea mist, with no engine, no loran, no steerer, no electrics, there's something in me that longs for a Mediterranean landfall where the visibility is so good and the mountains so high it seems you're never more than a few hours from seeing something you recognize.

The breeze stays fresh, but there is more and more mist in it. We start giving foghorn signals. There are no fishing boats to hear. We click off six and a half to seven knots by the hour. Our deep-sea routine remains unchanged, but this close to land it begins to feel cramped.

On soundings! The depth sounder was reading infinity. Now it comes up to ninety fathoms. It intrigues me that they used soundings long before depth sounders. Sounding the depths with weights and string. You can drown in six inches, I remind the crew, but being on soundings is a morale boost nonetheless. Sixty miles to go!

Through the mist comes rain driven by twenty-knot winds. The double head rig keeps the boat driving well. Double neck towels and rubber bands at the wrists and ankles don't do as well keeping me dry. Dribbles down your neck are bad, but into your armpit . . .

For the last hour Chris has been hopping . . . taking radio nulls, checking the Walker log, bugging us every ten minutes for "course steered," taking the depth, working over his chart. Even if he knew where we are he'd be working this hard. Have we been set by the current? How much leeway or sideward drift have we made under sail? How good is our speed estimation? After taking aim something like three hundred miles ago, where will we hit Ireland?

We've been aiming at Tory Island. A bit either way and we're still close to our course on to Oban and the canal. Halfway down the companionway, his sou'wester a bit askew, Chris asks me, "What do you think we've got for visibility?"

"Quarter mile at worst. Don't worry. That still gives us time enough to put on the brakes."

Tone has been taking longer tricks at the wheel while I try to help Chris. There's not much that I can do, but two heads sometimes can help. I wonder, though, when Chris goes topside to sniff the wind.

"If you want real Irish navigation, lad, take a bucket of potatoes to the bow. Throw one off every thirty seconds or so. When one of them doesn't splash . . . *stop*."

"Thanks, Bels. Thanks a lot."

We're within five miles now. You can see the tops of the waves changing shape; the backwash from the surf has some small effect even out here. These are not the deep-sea waves we've been seeing for the past few days. I'm beginning to think I was being too generous estimating our visibility.

"Let's get the staysail down and put in a reef to slow her down some," I say to Tone. None of us has been off watch for the past six hours. Chris sticks his head up and sniffs again.

"Can you smell Guinness?" Tone chirps.

"I . . . I just thought I smelled hay."

Land!

Right at the rim of our visibility . . . hills, cliffs, closer than I'd have thought. Waves breaking, too.

"Is that the island, Chris?" Tone asks.

"I don't know. It looks too high, too big for the island. It could easily be the Irish coast. I'm pretty sure it's not one of the Hebrides. If we're off, we're probably off to the south. I think it makes sense to take some sail off and close a bit more with the coast until we can pick up something."

"Okay. I don't want to be any closer under those cliffs than we have to, though."

"You're right," said Chris. Then, after consulting the chart, the pilot, and the RDF, he says, "This is the Irish coast. Tory Island has to be out to port somewhere."

And it was. Chris guided us into the coast just south of Arran Island, less than five miles below our course for Tory Island and then on to Oban.

"The radio makes it pretty easy," he said about the squiggly abstract lines he'd been able to pluck from the BBC and other fine navigational sources.

"Bullshit," said Tone. "I saw how easy it was. That was beautiful. That was great." And she and I stumbled over ourselves to hug the navigator.

Just past dinner we reached around the top of Ireland in parting mist clouds shot through with glimpses of the setting sun. The breeze began to leave us, so, while we had daylight enough to reassemble the system, we tackled the slumbering engine. Fingers and toes were crossed. It waited for us to start it in the conventional way—no sizzling battery terminals, no other surprises. Then it started! Now, did we have fuel enough for a hundred miles?

The Firth of Lorne is lovely . . . very like a fjord. A spectacular knife-cut of water right into the middle of Scotland. We're powering into it now through morning mist that may well burn off to let us appreciate it. Tone breaks out her pipe.

We can see clear sky overhead, but the mist on the water gets denser. We have found the channel marks and are on a good range, but it still would be nice to see. To starboard, Tone sees something. Breakers!

"Closer than I thought," says Chris, and sends us back to port a bit. Channel or not, I keep stretching my eyes into the fog as we power on.

Throttle back to conserve fuel or press on to make Oban before dark? I say press on, while Chris points at a seal popping out of our wake. When we turn and look ahead again, there is Oban.

"Closer than I'd thought," I mutter to myself.

We glide into the miniature basin. We find no space, so we coast alongside another boat and kill the engine. We've made it! When we cut the engine we can all hear, coming through the stillness of the Scottish evening, the high clear sound of bagpipes.

Chapter Twenty-three

Oscarsborg . . . the fort, the little island, the entrance to the strait, the passage on up to Oslo . . . Oscarsborg is on the bow. Almost home. We're almost there. *Tresbelle* has been voyaging, so have I, but three more miles and we're under the guns of the fortress, fifteen more miles and we're at our mooring.

High puffy clouds over the land, a ten-knot breeze on the port bow. It's a rare day. We've come around from Flekkefjord. I say "we." Chris and Tone went ashore there. I sailed singlehanded to Kristiansand; Arne Five and Mike Høye joined me there for the sail up the Skagerrak, into the Oslofjord, and home.

Work caught up with my Atlantic shipmates. Both Chris and Tone had to get to work. I tried to kid them into recalculating their priorities, I tried to get them to finish the voyage with me, but they had to go. It was a rushed goodbye. We arrived at the quay in Flekkefjord about 1700. They were gone on the 1930 train. Of course, they're not really "gone." I'll see them again, but the end of a voyage is a milestone. It feels very different not to have them aboard. I couldn't say goodbye calmly. They know me well, they saw my tears. What friends!

But back in Oban, at the end of our transatlantic crossing, the mood had been very different. We'd been talking about pubs—our favorite ones and our love for each of them—and about ales and scones and high teas, ever since we first decided, way out there somewhere in the murk off the Grand Banks, to head for Scotland. The bagpipes hadn't died away before we were ashore from our salty, half-stowed home. Arm in arm, down the Quayside street we went, maybe a hundred meters before Chris spied the Three Crowns, and we had found a home ashore. Claire the publican, Albie, Cameron, and Arnold at the bar, all used to voyagers but the soul of Scotland all the same. Our sea legs still betraying us every so often, we told them our tall tales, and there was much more than an ale or two to fuel us as we went along. The flushed, grateful, drained, mellow feeling of having made it, made it together through runaway trawlers, dolphin displays, and a few million waves . . . that feeling is why we'd gone sailing to begin with. Or so it seemed.

One of the late arrivals asked me where we'd sailed from.

"Boston."

"Goin back tinite, arrre ye?"

I laughed confusedly, then laughed some more when I found out that there's a port nearby named Boston. I was just as happy not to have to worry about navigating even that far tonight.

In the safety of *Tresbelle*'s galley, though, after weathering the perils of a transatlantic crossing and the walk home, I suffered my worst injury of the voyage: I chopped a chunk off the end of my finger while making dinner. Unfortunate, sloppy, bloody, and inconvenient, at least it set me free from washing the dishes. There's a certain carelessness that comes when you've "made it." Something like waiting to be the last person on the bus out of Neuengamme.

Tresbelle and we are again sliding homeward in perfect sailing weather with the sun crisp in the sky and scooped white clouds ringing the mountaintops around us, but sailing hasn't been that smooth all along. While we were in Oban, Archie Maxwell, the electrician, had done a diagnosis and repair, but we had a relapse complete with sizzling battery terminal the following day. Archie drove out along the canal system to find us, operated again at great length, and charged us practically nothing. Since then, we've had consistent electricity and a docile engine, but my confidence in the whole system is not very high. I hope Sigurd can sort it out and that it holds out until I get to him.

Taking the Caledonian Canal was a good idea, but we'd have had more fun exploring it if we'd been more relaxed for time. I was anxious now to return to Oslo in order to resolve all the uncertainties of my marriage and to meet my family. Otherwise sailing Loch Ness, tying up to trees, sampling haggis in the country pubs, and chatting with the lock keepers would have occupied more of my time. But Chris and Tone could spare no more time. I want to come back with Ellen.

Entering one of the locks under sail, I fouled up. In close quarters, I was undecided about which side of the lock to take. *Tresbelle* was halfway into a landing when the lock keeper waved me off. Instead of stopping and trying again, I headed for the downwind side. I hadn't thought it through. We grazed a moored boat, bumped the lock wall, and badly bent our bow pulpit. Tone was on the bow. She felt that someone stronger could have fended off better. I reminded her that *Tresbelle* weighs seven tons.

Setting the spinnaker out in the North Sea: Chris and Tone had never done it themselves. They didn't call me up; it was blowing fifteen or so; Chris took the halyard, the sail filled with wind halfway up, and it lifted him off the deck. Before being sucked to the top of the mast he let the halyard run and was fine except for fists full of nasty rope burns.

"Just think, Tone, if you'd been fending off, now all three of us would be wearing bandages."

"You looked pretty funny heading for the spreaders," she retorted.

Now we're approaching the strait. Beneath its surrounding heights, the breeze is blocked almost completely. Only little tendrils of wind swirl down to us to put prints of ripples on the sound's surface. During the calm stretches, *Tresbelle* stands up straight, gliding, sails nearly slack. She slows, wavers as she loses steerage, then hangs limp and slows to a stop.

A puff arrives. The sweat on my neck cools, the boat tips, wiggles back toward course, and moves again. The bow cuts water, and wavelets start lapping like a rock breaking a stream. This isn't a surfing pace, but it isn't the doldrums. There's wind, you just have to find it. If I were more confident in it, I'd think about starting the engine, but I'm actually just as happy to slide home silently, to enjoy the homecoming by myself while my crew dozes undisturbed below.

Close beneath the fort we glide by the smooth stone walls. There are the big guns. They look like giraffes—more like long-necked clams, actually—sitting aloof up there. There's the torpedo battery, the tops of the disused tubes just visible under-water. In the hills off to starboard behind the sails were the shore batteries. No mist in the channel, sun-warmed hills with no wet snow . . . it's not April, certainly not April 9, 1940.

The sails come aback. The boat is standing straight. Sailing between these hills you just have to hold on. The jib has no wind in it. It snakes against the shrouds. The main boom slides and slats. There is no wind in our sails at all. The wheel is lifeless, and the boat starts to spin slowly like a log in the fol-lowing current. A dark crosshatch of ripples slides out toward us from the fort. There are no other boats, no people ashore. The gateway to Oslo is ours. The jib fills, the main slides to leeward . . . a gentle heel, astern the vee of a wake . . . *Tres-belle* eases past the fortress into the strait beyond. Aeolus's bag mustn't quite be cinched tight.

The spot where the *Blücher* sank is just to port, just ahead. Sometimes, on calm days, you can see a wisp of diesel oil on the surface. I see a few small rainbows of seepage now. I think of the hulking bones of that ship, of the bones of men that must still be inside. Drifting here above the *Blücher* I think of those drowned sailors. The grins of those corpses Ragnvald and I stacked in Dachau, the waves from Jon, Per, and Lars, their "See you later," the vacant steering-house windows of that trawler. I've sailed over the *Blücher* before. Those men had come to enslave us. It was them against us. They had to die.

We sank them, they occupied us. They had their already dead, they had the final solution, they had the dogs and whips to use on us. Why not? We were not people. We were not "them." We were not "them" and that's how they could do what they did to us.

How could we not hate the death's-head helmets, the obscene tanks, the gallows, the capos? How could we not hate the marines crouched behind the *Blücher*'s armor panting to leap ashore and arrest the king or to kill him? We had to hate them to survive, and we did, but we can't anymore . . . or at least I can't anymore. What makes war work is the opposition of "them" to "us." Hating those bastards keeps it going around just the way Goebbels made it go around. Because of nuclear bombs, sure, but also because of the cherry-red chimney on the cre-matorium at Natzweiler, that chain must be broken. I fear that it won't be. It never has been. There are more people interned without trial in the world today than the Nazis ever held in concentration camps. After us, after our children even, could come a deluge of "us" enslaving "them," of "them" annihi-lating "us." The only way to stop that is to create one big "us." Everyone should realize that. Who can't see what we've done to each other? What we can do? But gliding over the buried *Blücher*, I'm feeling new stirrings attached to that old knowl-edge. My stubborn heart slides a bit. I look down and I think and feel and say to the drowned sailors, "My brothers." From where I've been, in coming home, I say it. This time there's no hollowness, no hypocrisy, no fear. The room for love, it seems, may even be there.

Tresbelle's sails come full aback. In the long lull that follows, her bow circles toward the rocks to starboard. I kick the wheel over. I scull the rudder four or five times. I have minimal control. To weather, I can see only glassy water. We have room. We won't hit the rocks, but this may be the end of sailing. I want to keep sailing.

The sails fill now, but from the back. The wind is blowing exactly the opposite way from two minutes ago. It's the downdraft off the hill. It fills in when there's a lull in the real breeze. It spins us slowly back to port, back away from the rocks, back into the channel. We're headed down the fairway. The sails go limp. There's no air at all; then there's a breath. *Tresbelle* hangs, immobile. I think of her reflection in the water, of the stars reflected in the deep-sea water. We can wait. I look up the hills and find the shore batteries. The cannons look like browsing bears. From directly abeam, angling a bit across our bow, comes a puff.

"Aeolus, *s'il vous plaît!*"

I can't do anything. The edge of the puff just catches us. *Tresbelle* shudders; quickly, she builds a miniature train of waves. The puff is just enough. We slide through the remainder of the narrows and out from under the hills. Once we're in wider water, there's clear air.

I leave the helm for a minute to wake Mike. He grumps out of his bunk, stumbles and bumps around the cabin, takes his time in the head, but when he surfaces to join me in the cockpit, he brings a cold beer. I tip the first two swallows into the Oslofjord as thanks to Aeolus.

Mike looks at me. "Giving Poseidon his due, I see," he says. "Home," he toasts.

"Home."

Chapter Twenty-four

Silly people. People being silly and it's not even a weekend. When I saw the flotilla, that's what I thought. Four or five of the boats I should have recognized. I was caught, still, in thoughts of the past, thoughts of passing the strait under sail, of leaving Boston, of begging the favors of Aeolus. As *Tresbelle* reached up the Oslofjord, fifteen or twenty boats rounded the corner. For a moment, it didn't register. Then I saw *Skarv*, Finn's boat. I'd sailed five Skaw races on her—I should have recognized her.

Finn and I had been friends ever since I started sailing. We'd raced and cruised and covered the waterfront together. In the war, he was a flying-boat pilot. When he came back, his uniform and glamorous adventures made him very much admired. Here was Finn leading the welcome for *Tresbelle*'s homecoming. It made a difference, a big difference. I was touched. It was the fleet of the Norwegian Ocean Racing and Cruising Club (Arne Brun Lie, past commodore). My friends! Some of them were the best sailors anywhere. They'd done so many things, and they were here doing fleet maneuvers, waving flags, and shooting off that silly cannon from the Colin Archer boat *Christiania* . . . all for *Tresbelle* and me. All I could think of to do was wave and laugh and cry quite a lot.

"Marching home" up with Karl Johans Gate with my cardboard suitcase at Ragnvald's limping pace, I felt no such excitement or jubilation. Back then, after being rescued from the camps, I think there were two problems: I didn't know whether to feel proud or ashamed, and I had virtually no feelings at all of any kind. It may have taken forty-some years, but it seems to me that my feelings have returned.

I can even pinpoint the time when I started to feel again. It was a day that Norwegians all remember: June 7, 1945. June 7 is the day commemorating our independence from Sweden. It was also the day, in 1940, when King Haakon proclaimed a truce and was evacuated to London. And it was on that day in 1945, exactly five years later, that he returned home. He was aboard the same ship, HMS *Devonshire*, that had taken him from Tromsö just ahead of the Nazis at the opening of our war.

I wasn't planning to go see the king disembark. Why go and feel out of place, feel like a stranger? I guess it was mostly curiosity that made me change my mind and find a place by the harbor. Even simple curiosity is some sign of life. When I got to the waterfront in Oslo, everybody else in Norway was there, too.

It was a beautiful day. The breeze was soft, from the south, and the smoke from the *Devonshire* rose straight above her, as if by magic, as if she weren't moving, as she steamed up the Oslofjord into the roadstead.

There were flags everywhere, and flowers. There is a sort of natural amphitheater, formed by the way the harborsides climb up and back from the waterfront. Thousands and thousands of people were perched around that curve. The launch, carrying the royal family, approached. Silence. Total silence as King Haakon approached. He stepped onto Norwegian soil for the first time in five years. I could hear the gasps and sobs. Crown Prince Olav had been in Oslo since the middle of May. He met the king. They saluted, and the silence gave way to a cheer, so united and spontaneous that I can still hear it. Haakon and his family rode the length of the waterfront. Then he mounted to the palace balcony. Tall, more haggard-looking than when he left, his uniform loose around his neck, he came to the rail.

I wept.

Some of the pegs that hold things together were being driven back in place. But I still drifted and brooded and felt out of place almost all the time. They had a big funeral for my friends. They found the ditch where they'd been shot. Their remains were cremated, and I laid Jon's ashes to rest myself. All of Oslo came. This was within days of the king's return. I was ashamed, but I shed no tears. My best friend. What the hell had happened to me? Before the Stapo snatched me from my room, I was scared to death wondering what might happen to Jon. Standing here, his ashes in my hand, why didn't I feel anything? Is that why I have the nightmare about his death?

Much of what was wrong with me was physical. Malnutrition, the aftereffects of typhus, tubercular pleurisy . . . I wasn't well. But I think, too, that my soul was confused. The camps filled me with so much hate that I choked on it. My shredded, paralyzed feelings had gone into hibernation. I had been a school boy when they dragged me away. I was older than old when I came back. Whatever the phrase means, "dealing with" what happened to me took a hell of a long time. I went into the sanitarium. It did more for my body than my soul. Then I broke free to go sailing. That gave me a real lift. Confusing as sailing can be, it was a simple challenge compared to putting myself together. I loved it, though, and it was sailing six-meter boats that made my sleeping soul start to stretch and wake up.

In Ottobrun, we were sixty-one Norwegians. We thought the war might end the next day when British Mosquito bombers staged a raid right outside our gates. But the war continued, and just twenty of that group survived to see Oslo again. We were sixteen when we off-loaded at Schirmeck in the Alsace. Of that Cell 27 group, just a few made it back. Those early months and years after the war were lonely.

That made it even better to see Ian Hopper. That was in 1948, at Farm Corner, a country house in Norfolk, England. I remember it well for my time with Ian, but also for fresh vegetables and fruit—exquisite *petits pois*, gooseberries, quinces, obscenely plump strawberries. And, yes, for ham—smoked ham, cured ham—and bacon. For turkey—stuffed, roasted, and smoked. Ah, smoked turkey! And for chickens—roasters and capons. And all the while there was food rationing throughout the United Kingdom.

I was in tanning and shoemaking school at Northampton College of Technology. On weekends I'd take the train to King's Lynn Station. There, in his old MG, would be Ian Hopper. He was recuperating at Farm Corner, and there I recuperated too on weekends and during vacations.

We did maintenance work around the place. We went to the beach, where the tide went out for miles. We played tennis. But most of all, we ate. When we'd had our ham and bacon and turkey and eggs and chicken and fruit with cream for breakfast, we would plan lunch.

When we talked about the camps we might joke about how bad we'd looked or how scared we'd been or what pigs the guards were. Being with Ian brought back the same sort of cheeky, desperate, insane fighting spirit that saved us. Ian's hands shook badly. He had nightmares. He still couldn't work. He had red pills and yellow pills and blue pills. Sometimes he was delightful; sometimes he seemed to disappear under a blanket . . . of chemicals, of nervous reaction? I loved to be with him, even more because he who had saved me so often now needed me.

We had a wizened, sprightly lady who came in to bake pies. Ian liked rhubarb, but the season was so short we wondered if we couldn't dry it and let Mary do her wonders all round the calendar. With great hanging racks, an elaborate rhubarb press, and a fair amount of hilarity, we managed to tuck away a bale of dried rhubarb. Unfortunately it rotted before we could reconstitute it. However, Mary made an Irish stew that kept us talking for weeks—a pastry top, chunks of meat and potatoes and carrots, and a gravy that was richer than Croesus. We were smacking our lips and patting full stomachs and talking about this Irish stew one evening when the call from Jan Naerup came. Ragnvald had died.

He had been studying medicine in Denmark. It was the injury from the kick to his spine. Somehow it had become tubercular. When the disease broke out, it just carried him away in a week.

Ragnvald! You were bent over between two bunks. The SS man didn't say "Achtung!" He just marched in. You had your head down. You, who were nothing if not a survivor, you who knew when to listen, when to get up, you didn't hear him. You simply didn't hear. The SS man went to you and planted his toe in your spine . . . and then the son of a bitch made you stand at attention. First your leg, then your back, now you're dead. Damn!

I can't think who could have helped me more that night than Ian. I wept over Ragnvald. The boy. The innocent. The survivor who did not survive in the end. Oh, Ragnvald. I felt a tremendous loneliness.

Of the four friends sent to NN camps in Germany in connection with the disastrous raid in Oslo, I was now the only one alive.

Europe's too small, the world's too small, to avoid having to live and deal with the Nazi bastards. The Nuremberg trials were sweet, in a way, but they were a circus. They almost made me sympathize with the monsters on trial.

I've been to Germany only a few times since I was released from Dachau. I've tried to avoid it. I've met Germans, of course, traveling. Some would see the Norwegian license plates on my car. "Oh, I was in Norway during the war. We had such a good time. It is such a beautiful country." Yes . . . in Norway for five years, and who invited you?

Right after the war there was a part of Jutland, a part of Germany, that was a military zone—occupied territory. It was occupied by Norwegians! I drove through there once. I can't say that I didn't enjoy it.

Cruising with friends on the Norwegian coast, I walk a beach, look up at a hill, and am surprised by the ruins of a Nazi bunker. I'm surprised, too, when, taken unawares, I feel physically sick.

Ten years after the war, I was a witness in a war-crimes trial. On trial was a Polish SS officer from Dautmergen. I recognized him—not at first, but I recognized him. That was my role in the trial. I think that he was accused of mass murder and that he got off with something like ten years because it was too late under German law to execute him. I don't favor capital punishment, so that was okay with me.

But then there were the people I met while it was going on. In the corridors, between sessions, several came up to me.

"You're lying," they said. "Those camps were never like that. They never murdered people. It's just propaganda from the Allies."

"Well, where are all of my friends? Friends who went into the camps with me but never came out? Are they still alive, you think?"

"Ah, you see how he lies," one woman said. "We suffered in the terror bombings. The planes dropped bombs on us. Our friends, our families were killed. Who puts those pilots on trial? Why should they be free?"

I tried to stay calm.

There were one or two Germans, even an SD guard, who showed some human feelings. I guess that just goes to show that it is possible. What about all of the others? What about the ones who caused us agony for their own pleasure? What about the ones at Neuengamme who, after we'd boarded our buses and were gone, loaded ten thousand prisoners, mostly Russians, onto barges and scuttled them? So far as I've learned, there were no survivors—and nearly on the last day of the war!

There aren't any excuses, any real answers, that I know. As human beings, we can't afford to consider the Germans a race of friends. But is there another answer?

When we were weathered in at Helgoland in February of 1979, delivering *Tresbelle* to the Amsterdam Boat Show, the coast guard captain who had "rescued" us on the way in invited us aboard his ship for dinner. The younger guys in my crew all wanted to go, but I said no.

"I don't mean to be impolite, but the Germans killed many of my friends in the war. I was treated very badly in concentration camps. These are things that I can't forget," I told the skipper.

"I am only thirty years old," he said. "I wasn't born when the things you're talking about happened. I had nothing to do with them, and neither did my crew. Please come aboard."

I felt silly and stubborn and old. I gave in.

The ladderway below into the ship seemed to descend forever—down two decks to an area forward, close to the waterline, with no portholes. Around a table formed to the curve of the hull were settees and padded couches covered with nut-brown leather. The deck beams overhead were capped with mahogany, and oak cabinets were fitted to the hull. Pictures hung on the bulkheads—rowing shells, hunting trophies, soccer teams, fishermen with trout. It seemed more like a shooting lodge than a ship's saloon.

When we were seated, glasses filled with vodka, the skipper said, "Come then onto my ship and leave behind what is in the past. *Prosit.*"

"Well, we're more than grateful to you," I answered. "For your hospitality as well as your seamanship. *Prosit!*"

Each of the others present then framed some sort of toast. I felt I was at a state banquet . . . fencing and probing. It was nothing like our 'brothers-of-the-sea' feelings of the night before when we'd come in out of the blizzard and the surf. I suppose most of that difference was my fault. Yes, these Germans had all been unborn when their fathers did what they did. *Prosit.*

Do you know what *Prosit* means? "May it be advantageous." A typically Teutonic toast?

Come on, Bels, I told myself, maybe you hate this phony Bismarck bull, but you brought it on yourself.

There were more toasts. Both the vodka and the stiffness began to disappear. Finally I rose to answer my friend and host.

"My apologies, but I believe that none of us can say, 'I had nothing to do with the Nazis'—not even you guys who weren't born then. The Nazis were human beings like all of us, so we have to admit that Nazism came from the human heart. That's why we're all involved—in understanding it, in burying it, in driving a stake through it. Your generation, especially, must understand, not forget. If we say the Nazis were monsters and not like us good guys, we're still involved, because we must stop the vengeance, the righteousness, that splinters us into 'good guys' and 'bad guys.' If we keep that up there won't be any of us left. None of us is an island. The sea divides us, but it binds us, too. I think the same thing is true about the depths of the human heart. Thank you for having us aboard."

The Eichmann trial, and more recently the conviction of "Ivan the Terrible"—these events scare and depress me. When there is jeering and cheering at the news that a man will die, even a monster of a man, how can we tell the monsters apart?

In 1979, I met a man named Odd Ronning from the Museum of the Norwegian Resistance Movement. He was interviewing survivors of the Nazi concentration camps. He called and asked if he could interview me.

"Your name?"

"Arne Brun Lie."

"Where born?"

"Oslo."

And so forth. He was straightforward. He knew how to probe, and I found myself talking at length. The heart of the interview was the part about the raid that my group was on and that led to our arrest.

Q: Yes . . . and someone succeeded in destroying the files and the building?

A: The building was not destroyed. Kirkevein 90 is a biggish apartment building. I think the person who had the files in his flat was named Kielland. I also know that he was absent and that some neighbor across the street saw fire in the Kiellands' flat, and this neighbor was a Nazi. He alerted the Stapo in their barracks, not far away. I think this is the way everything was discovered. Then there was quite a lot of shooting, and Per Stranger-Thorsen and Jon Hatland, who were keeping guard outside, were caught. They were armed but had never actually been able to use—to practice with—the arms. Max Manus [one of Norway's greatest heroes, the man who sank the transport *Donau* with limpet mines and made havoc for the Nazis wherever he went] was one of our instructors and was on the raid. Gregers Gram [another instructor and a great pal of Max Manus;

he was killed a few months later in another action] and Dick
[Dick Zeiner-Henriksen, code-named Stein—Erik's brother and
the leader of our group] shot their way out of a corridor in the
building and got away. Roy Nilsen, another of our instructors,
was not on the raid. He was killed with Gregers. Hans Petter
Styren was hit by several bullets, but got outside and hid himself in a pile of wood till morning came. A man came by, and
H.P.S. emerged from his hiding with his Colt .45 and said,
"You must help me, and if you don't, I am afraid I will have
to shoot you." And it so happened that the man was a doctor,
and above all, he was deeply engaged in the resistance. H.P.S.
was taken care of and later sent to Sweden.

Q: "Had the necessary luck in unluck," as they say? You knew
about the raid but didn't participate. It is tempting to ask how
the connection was made. What do you know about this today?

A: It is still a puzzle to me. I may have been shadowed. Someone
may have broken down. I was in their class. Who knows? I'm
afraid that I don't.

The interview proceeded in much the same vein. When it
was over, I felt terrible. I'd been coughing up facts to be ana-
lyzed (without, it seemed, much real understanding), facts which
I'd been chasing ever since the Stapo broke down my door in
1944. Those pieces of information that were passed along so
quickly and questioned from such strange angles were gathered from people no longer alive, people in camps, people I
met in strange places long after the war. What had happened
on the Kirkeveien 90 raid? I'd been asking that question for
years. Now I was a "source," maybe even the only source.

Had somebody from our group compromised me?

I didn't know. Was there a "fact" missing to explain why I
was sent to the camps?

It may be coincidence, but I didn't start having nightmares
until after the interview.

Q: One last question. Have you run across people who now try to
minimize what went on in the camps, people who say that

Natzweiler never existed? As an NN prisoner, what are your feelings when you hear these things?

A: One has to pinch one's arm and to ask oneself if one was really there. Was it all as I thought? Of course, yes. It is an impossibility to imagine something like that. The smell, for example. When I visited Natzweiler five years ago, it was a dreadful and emotional experience. I remembered everything. If I exist, Natzweiler existed.

I was on a business trip in the Alsace. We were looking at shoe factories. I wasn't thinking of anything in particular when I saw a sign for Schirmeck. A stab like an icicle to the groin, a punch to the solar plexus. I was truly surprised.

I told my friends I had been there in the war.

"Natzweiler?"

"You've heard of it?"

"Yes, I have. There's a museum there. It's not far away. Why don't we go?"

I wasn't sure. Finally, curiosity overcame my hibernation reflex. We went through the museum. It included just two barracks, the crematorium, and the gallows. Pictures gave some sense of how it was, but that mix of shit and sweat and burning flesh was in my nostrils alone. What to say? I lost much of my curiosity very quickly. Just as before, all I wanted was to get out.

My friends didn't know what to expect from me. I had no idea what to tell them. We started back down the mountain.

"Stop here, please."

The chimney, painted gray now and splotched with rust, still stood out against the slope. I got back in the car. I didn't say a word for the rest of the four-hour drive.

The questions I couldn't answer, the difference between the way it was and my ability to describe it, procrastination, real life, fear, and the clumsy feel of a pen in my hands—all those things kept me from writing my story. The years went by, comrades passed on, all around me were people who knew nothing of the camps. Stumbling blocks are there, but my need to speak grew.

Then I met Ellen. I was living near Boston, and had businesses on both sides of the Atlantic. My marriage had fallen apart, into separation. Ellen quickly became my main reason for rolling the camps into a ball, for passing something along out of the war. I made some stabs at it, doomed three-page efforts. And then I went sailing "home to Oslo" aboard *Tresbelle*.

My homecoming from the camps was gray, quaky, and bittersweet. Arrival in Oslo aboard *Tresbelle*, because it tied so many parts of me together and mostly because it capped a challenge that strained me, that intrigued me, and that helped bury some stubborn ghosts, was almost the opposite. Confusion was replaced now with purpose, quakiness with a sense of strength. My crossing was a milestone and more.

I married Ellen and I started the book.

I took a draft to Elie Wiesel, who teaches at Boston University and whose works, especially those about his time as a concentration camp prisoner, have inspired me. He treated me "like a brother," which was flattering, and I left a copy of what I'd written with him. After receiving Wiesel's help and counsel and his message to "guard the flame," I went home and lit into writing. I also looked for more Wiesel to read. Near the end of *Messengers of God* I found:

I was preoccupied with Job, especially in the early years after the war. In those days he could be seen on every road of Europe. Wounded, robbed, mutilated. Certainly not happy, not resigned. I was offended by Job's surrender in the (Biblical) text. He should not have given in so easily. He agreed to go back to living as before. Therein lay God's true victory: He forced Job to welcome happiness. . . . Job did not hesitate or procrastinate. By repenting sins he did not commit, by justifying a sorrow he did not deserve, he communicates to us that he did not believe in his own confessions. Job personified man's eternal quest for justice and truth—he did not choose resignation. Thus he did not suffer in vain; thanks to him, we know it is given to man to transform divine injustice into human justice and compassion.

For survivors, such flashes of meaning come all too infrequently. Certainly the despair at the center of our suffering is powerful. Primo Levi's suicide seems to me just one of a number of victories for that dark side. But accepting the suffering and letting it open life is still a possibility. I have worried long that my optimism might be foolish, that my attempts to "move on" might be superficial. Wiesel has helped me lay some of those doubts to rest.

My father was in the leather business, and I have been too for a long time. Now, though, I'm on the edge of something more. Mike Linquata, my partner, used to work in his father's Gloucester fish-packing plant. "You know, Dad, even though you pay me nothing, I'm happy," he told his old man. "If it weren't for me, there would be a hundred thousand fewer meals in the world every week."

Mike and I, with some other friends, are embarking on a fish-farming venture, the first of its kind in North America. With luck enough and help from Aeolus and Poseidon, we hope to produce a hundred thousand meals a day.

Ellen is more than someone to calm me after my bad dreams. She's young enough to appreciate the virtues of an experienced fellow like myself. She's the critic who holds my ramblings about deep-sea adventures and concentration camp life to believability, and she's the mother of Siv.

"Poppa Arne" is what my little girl calls me. Already she can steer *Tresbelle* a bit. When she was born, it seemed at first a reluctant entry into the world. Ellen's contractions weren't, evidently, strong enough to dilate her cervix. After waiting for nature to take its course, the doctor finally introduced odd objects. I forget the technical name that he used for them, but he said, "They're just sticks of seaweed." They worked, the birth went beautifully, and so my Viking daughter came into this world with seaweed in her hair. *Siv* in Norwegian means "reed."

WGBH, the public television station in Boston, recently aired an exhaustive French documentary on the concentration camps. I didn't know whether to watch it or not. After the first episode I felt drained, and bad dreams kept me from getting much sleep. On the second night I found it unbearable. There was lots of testimony from contemporary Germans: "Yes, I knew the trains went to Auschwitz, but it was my job to schedule them, not to know what they carried."

Over and over, this sort of excuse from the people interviewed twisted at my insides. Still, this time, nestled on my chest was my infant daughter. I squeezed Ellen's hand, hugged Siv close, and thought to myself: This is it. *Here I am*. That's my revenge.

Index